A Love That Heals

A Love That Heals

Edward E. Thornton

Editor

Unless otherwise indicated, Scripture quotations are from *The New Testament, a Translation in the Language of the People,* by Charles B. Williams. Copyright 1937 and 1966. Moody Press, Moody Bible Institute of Chicago. Used by permission. Quotations marked GNB are from the *Good News Bible,* the Bible in Today's English Version. Old Testament: Copyright © American Bible Society 1976; New Testament: Copyright © American Bible Society 1966, 1971, 1976. Used by permission. Quotations marked RSV are from the Revised Standard Version of the Bible, copyrighted 1946, 1952, © 1971, 1973. Quotations marked KJV are from the King James Version of the Bible.

Dewey Decimal Classification: 242.4
Subject Headings: CONSOLATION//MEDITATIONS
Library of Congress Catalog Card Number: 83-21083
Printed in the United States of America

Library of Congress Cataloging in Publication Data

Thornton, Everett W.
   A love that heals.

   1. Meditations.   I. Thornton, Edward E.   II. Title.
BV4832.2.T524 1984   242   83-21083
ISBN 0-8054-5105-6 (pbk.)

Contents

Editor's Preface

The spiritual journey recorded in these pages gathered dust for a quarter of a century. The author, Everett Thornton, is my father. Sometime in the mid-1950s he sent the manuscript to me as a way of sharing his journey, and also asking my opinion regarding its suitability for publication. He was in his early sixties, I in my early thirties.

I was pleased that he was coping with the aftermath of several heart attacks so well, but his issues were not mine. He was relinquishing a career, I was intent on establishing one. He was facing death, I was earning a doctorate in theology. He was discovering the living Christ; I the sciences of human behavior. He was centered on the inner life—one's real self and the union of the self with God; I was concentrating on dressing my ego in professional competence and credentials.

True to my professional standards, I sought a second opinion about publication. I responded, then, with many words— words of appreciation, reservation, recommendation for revision, and so forth. Had all the words been boiled down into their essence, however, my reply would have been one big *no*. Subsequently, a publisher also said *no*.

In the meantime twenty-five years passed by. I established my career as a pastoral specialist, entered the mid-life period with diminishing spiritual authenticity, suffered a health crisis of my own, encountered death—and was encountered by the living Presence as well! Then, Everett Thornton had a final heart attack, lingered a few weeks and died—thirty years after the first attack which launched him on the spiritual journey recorded here.

A few months later Verdelle Case Thornton followed her husband in death. In closing their house, I found my father's manuscript—and remembered.

Remembering stirred surprise more than regret. I was surprised at my excitement about traveling his journey with him, seeing what he saw, and allowing his journey to inform mine. I was surprised, too, by his title, "Spiritual Journey." For the past several years I had developed my teaching of the psychology of religious experience around the theme: the spiritual journey. I thought the words, as well as the slant, were original with me. But there they were on the binder of a fat loose-leaf notebook: "Spiritual Journey (Revised)"—and I remembered. Remarkable, I thought, how empty the phrase felt to me in my thirties and how rich with meaning and exciting with promise now that I am nearly the age that his journey began. One of his meditations provides the title for the material in published form: *A Love That Heals.* My father's spiritual journey was a healing journey as well.

Two years later, having worked through most of the stages in the grief process, I packed the manuscript and brought it with me to the Indiana woods on vacation. I reread it for remembering. *Perhaps,* I said to myself, *if the essays warrant it, I may do a private edition for the grandchildren and a few special friends of the family.* One thing seemed sure, I was not going to push one more personal story of coping with a mid-life crisis onto the book-buying public.

Memory had played another trick on me. As I entered these pages, I discovered more than one man's story. To be sure, the author's personal pain and struggle and process of transformation unfold. But the journey is not focused on inner feelings and the details of a personal biography. The journey occurs in the pages of the Gospels where he discovered *a love that heals.* The central character is not Everett Thornton but the Jesus of history and the living Christ. The living Christ emerges from the pages of the New Testament—as available to the reader as he is to the author, regardless of the circumstances of one's life.

What dawned upon me was this: the spiritual journey I am seeing here is not merely the journey of a cardiac patient. It is not just the transition of a man through middle age. It is an account of a process of transformation from a life spread thin over many good things to a life centered in willing one thing, and that, loving God with a whole heart and one's neighbor as oneself. The transformation occurs without the aid of psychotherapist or spiritual director and without the direct involvement of friends or family. The transformation occurs slowly and silently in the process of regular, sincere attention to the Jesus of the Gospels and the still, small voice of the living Christ of experience.

The author tells us how it happens. He says, "The more I study about Jesus, the greater is my desire to understand him. These days [of postcardiac confinement] I am not reading my Testament from a sense of duty. I am driven by eagerness and desire." That is the clue: desire not duty. Each day he would read an entire Gospel through at one sitting. Then having read all four in four days, he would go back and reread them all again—over and over. He adds, "I never weary of the narratives. They amaze me with their freshness and vitality." Eventually, from the worn pages of his New Testament whose margins were filled with notes, emerged the clear, commanding, and compelling figure of Christ. The Christ discerned in this way and confirmed in the author's inner experience lives now in the pages that follow.

Readers of this volume need to be aware that, for the most

part, I left the verb tenses as my father wrote them in his notebook. He believed very strongly in and wrote on the basis of his present experiences with Jesus Christ. In one of the meditations he wrote: "The episodes in the Gospels in which Christ performs great works through faith had formerly seemed far away and unreal to me. Now they have come alive, and as my journey progresses, the people and happenings become very real. I find myself participating in the experiences of the disciples and listening to the words of Christ as though he were speaking directly to me." Leaving the present tense is a way of inviting readers to participate in this journey with Christ with my father as he shares his personal experiences.

Good things happen to the reader and fellow traveler who shares Everett Thornton's spiritual journey. Faith grows firm in the real presence and power of the living Christ to heal and to transform one's inner life. Hope awakens. I, at any rate, began to say to myself, "I too have found a pearl of great price, and I can make the life-style changes necessary to possess it." The stern face of loss softens, beckoning one into spiritual growth. Confidence grows: "I, too, can use experience of loss and limitation to help me reorder my priorities." *A Love That Heals* wakens longings to shift one's center from external to internal achievements, from material to spiritual treasures, and from extrinsic to intrinsic rewards in religious experience. Finally, one's way of loving is thrust into a smelting furnace where self-seeking melts away and only the desire to love God for God's sake, and for God's sake alone, survives.

Before long a reader knows at the center of his or her very being: "the key that unlocked the Scriptures for Everett Thornton will unlock them for me as well. The formula for overcoming hard circumstances will work for me, too." At the heart of each of us, as the author declares, "is an indestructable, inner, spiritual heart." We know it to be so when our own hearts leap again and again in a joyful realization of a new and transforming awakening in process as we, too, travel the spiritual journey.

So, I redoubled my editorial efforts, reneged on my promise not to seek a public reading audience, and prepared the record of my father's journey with Christ for an audience of many faces: (1) For convalescent middle-aged persons whose Christian experience, though sincere, has proved inadequate to cope with the insult of a major illness, a severe loss, or simply with the process of aging in the second half of life.

(2) For persons of whatever age or circumstance whose way of exercising faith in God is in transition. These are the people who are finding that a rational, critical, and thoroughly "sensible" (that is, safe and somewhat conventional) way of exercising faith is becoming threadbare. For them life itself is calling for an authentic, experiential faith, not necessarily a faith that fits the forms of organized religion, but a faith that feeds one with the experience of oneness with all that is, that joins one with the God in whom we live and move and have our being— an experience that transforms one's attitudes and relationships with others as well.

(3) For ministers and laypersons involved in the pastoral care of the persons described.

(4) For seminarians studying pastoral care in human crisis and seeking to understand and facilitate the transitions from one stage of faithing to another. Ultimately the teaching and learning of pastoral care is a process of understanding the spiritual journey of the care giver as well as those for whom the caring capacities of local congregations are organized. *A Love That Heals* both stimulates and informs that process.

My father's spiritual journey begins in an ambulance ride to a hospital in Shawnee, Oklahoma. Everett W. Thornton, fifty-seven, professor of history at Oklahoma Baptist University, is admitted to coronary care. Of the ambulance ride he writes, "I feel a distinct, certain knowing that I am going out there. I am afraid. I am in a state of panic. I know I am going out there. I know that suddenly I will meet him, and I wonder, *Is he friendly?*" In that ambulance, holding his hand, I sat—a middler seminarian, home for the holidays. What he does not write, and may well have forgotten, is that he voiced his fear to me, received some glib reassurance that, of course, God is friendly, and then sharply challenged me with the words, "How do *you* know?" And I was dumbstruck.

Thirty years later, at age eighty-seven, he lay in the Shawnee Medical Center during his final illness. We shared many deep things in those early morning hours before hospital routines intruded. On one occasion he recalled our ambulance ride thirty years before and said, "You know, many years later it came to me one day that Peter must have met me at the gate of heaven during that ambulance ride. He looked me over and gave his order: 'He's not a keeper. Throw him back. Maybe he will grow some more.'" Then, looking me in the eyes with quiet confidence and obvious enjoyment of the fishing imagery which he knew I would appreciate, he added, "And I know that I have grown spiritually in the thirty years since that day. I believe he will find me to be a keeper this time." And I said, "Thanks, Dad, for sharing your faith with me."

So that is what *A Love That Heals* is about. Growing spiritually. Becoming a "keeper." Knowing the answer to the ultimate spiritual question: Is God friendly? And then laying the book down saying, "Thanks, Everett, for sharing your faith with me."

EDWARD E. THORNTON
Wildridge
Birdseye, Indiana
August 3, 1982

Author's Preface

These essays were prepared mainly for Christians faced with the problem of readjusting their lives in the wake of a major misfortune. They reflect my own thoughts and feelings during such a time of difficult adjustment. The victorious outcome for me leads me to venture the hope that others with similar needs may gain spiritual help from the record of my experience.

Most of us are hesitant about revealing our religious experience. If we were more articulate in that respect, we could often be of help to one another. For that reason I have put modesty aside and have tried to provide a personal context for my discoveries.

It would of course be presumptuous for me to offer these studies in the name of biblical scholarship, a field in which I claim no special competence. *My one purpose is to witness to the restorative power of the Christian faith.* Therefore, the content sections themselves no less than the more personal meditations are intended as a sharing of experience. My prayer is that the reader shall have an experience of Christ in the inner life.

EVERETT W. THORNTON, 1956

1
Journey Begun

Is God Friendly?

God is love, and whoever continues to love continues in union with
God and God in union with him. . . . There is no fear in love, and
perfect love drives out fear (1 John 4:16*b*,18*a*).

I cannot say when I first entertained the thought that God
might *not* be friendly. But in flashes of comprehension I had
realized what a fearful possibility it would be. If we are only so
much protoplasm in a universe of cold unfeeling matter
controlled by forces which are wholly indifferent to us, what
then happens to all our hopes, our faith in God, and the
spiritual values which we experience? How, for example, can
we ourselves love if God does not love us? What of the sacred
relationships of friendship, loyalty, marriage? What becomes of
these spiritual values after death? Indeed, what fate awaits the
human spirit if we live in a universe indifferent to us?

But I pushed these fleeting fears aside. In truth I ran away
from them.

Then, suddenly, I could not run away any longer. The
question had to be faced, and faced immediately. And it
became the starting point of the spiritual journey with which
these pages deal.

It happened to me in a heart attack in my fifty-seventh year
(December 1951). When the attack begins, I feel a distinct,

certain knowing that I am going out there. I am afraid. I am in a
state of panic. I know I am going out there. I know that
suddenly I will meet him, and I wonder, *Is he friendly?* At once
the thought darts out, "Christ came to say he was friendly,"
but doubt crowds in: "What if Christ is mistaken? *Is God really
friendly?*" Here I am, suddenly stripped of all the trappings. I
am going out there. It is just my spirit, my real self. I am not
going to be there in body. I am about to leave that behind—
and go out there. And I wonder, *Is he really friendly? Is God
love?* I try to lean on the things I have been taught about God.
But I cannot lean on anything. I wonder about the place of
Jesus in all this. Perhaps I should not wonder, but I do. I am
going out there, and I wonder, *Is he friendly?*

It all happens in a few minutes, maybe ten or twenty—on
the ride in the ambulance. The feelings come back many times
in the critical days—those days before I know how it will come
out. Afterward, everything is different. I have faced death. I
have asked the ultimate question: "Is God friendly?"

For months I try to put things together. There is plenty of
time to think. I begin rereading the Gospels. I read what good
and wise men have to say about faith and the Christian hope. I
read again and again the penetrating letters of the great apostle
Paul. But most of all I live with Matthew, Mark, Luke, and
John. I enter into the mind and spirit of Christ. I become
certain about Jesus' place. I rediscover Christ.

Indeed, the whole journey is an experience in rediscovery.
Like the two disciples who encountered Jesus on the road to
Emmaus, I am not so much informed of new facts as
enlightened concerning things I have known all along. The
risen Lord, encountered as a living Presence, enables me to
see the meaning of the Scriptures just as he opened their eyes
on the Emmaus road to the meaning of the tragic events in
Jerusalem. As one writer points out, they became not more

learned but wiser. How fortunate that they were learned so that they could be made wiser!

So it is in my experience. My years of Bible study and Christian experience come to my aid. Certain values which had been in the foreground of my life recede, while others—spiritual values—move to the center. I had always honored them but now they take on new meaning and importance. I gain perspective. As I try on my new spiritual glasses a surprising thing happens: the figure of Christ comes into focus, clearer than I had ever seen it before. The kingdom of God appears as a challenging reality. The kingdom of God is in truth the mind of Christ. I move in eagerly to explore this marvelous kingdom of the spirit, and along the way I take copious notes. Hence, the words which follow, written as they were during periods of convalescence, could be called "Notes from My Devotional Hours." That hour, extended and unhurried during long periods of ill health, became a time of writing, as well as Bible reading.

Thus it is that these studies constitute a record of my spiritual journey with Jesus Christ. They are the highlights of experiences and insights as I roam through the rich pastures of the Gospel narratives. None is more important than the assurance which grew out of this initial experience, that Jesus is speaking the truth when he says that God is our Heavenly Father, one who cares. The Ruler of the universe is friendly. He is even more than a God of love. God himself *is* love.

> O love that wilt not let me go,
> I rest my weary soul in thee;
> I give thee back the life I owe,
> That in thine ocean depths its flow
> May richer, fuller be.
>
> —GEORGE MATHESON

Conquest of Fear

Everything is possible for him who has faith (Mark 9:23b).

I am coming to terms with the problem of fear—not the fear of physical pain or suffering, not the fear of God's judgment, but the fear of death. My entire philosophy of life, my Christian faith is at stake. I have to be honest with myself and admit that I am short on faith. Faith is the opposite of fear; when one is present the other must go. Faith drives out fear as light drives out darkness. But in my own life there is a mixture of both faith and fear. A weak faith must be made strong somehow. Initially, I prayed for more faith with which to overcome fear.

I am impressed by the way Jesus deals with fear, and by the frequency with which the subject appears in the Gospels. Over and over again Jesus urges people to rid themselves of fear. How? By trusting in God, the Heavenly Father. In that respect Jesus is simply sharing his own experience. He himself is absolutely free from fear of any kind because he is so fully conscious of God's presence with him in every moment of his life. With his trust in God's constant protection, there is nothing whatever to fear. It is this simple trust, and his sense of the Father's presence as real as the presence of his friends about him, which gives Jesus such complete assurance. Still, more important, he keeps telling the people that they can experience the same peace and happiness which he knows. He tells them how it can be had, namely, by entering with him into the kingdom of God.

Here is a powerful new motive for me to reexamine the teachings of Christ and explore the kingdom of God more fully than I have ever done. In order to overcome fear and doubt I am led to find out more about the inner life of the Master. I want to discover the secret wells of spiritual strength from which he draws tremendous power. I am not satisfied merely to say: "Jesus Christ was the Son of God, hence all this was to be expected of him." Is he not insisting on every page of the Gospels that I too can experience his joy in life, his freedom from fear, his fellowship with the Father? What Jesus is offering is a sort of "package proposition." It is a way of life, not merely a formula for overcoming fear or any other single problem.

Fear begins to fall away as I yield myself more fully to the whole message of Christ. Adversity, disappointments, and defeated hopes become actual advantages in attaining spiritual goals. I discover that I can more than compensate for a disabled physical heart with a profound awareness of the indestructability of the inner spiritual heart.

Many things enter into my growing conquest of fear. But the basic condition is the kind of trust which is evident in the life of Christ. Although I hasten to say with Paul that "I have not yet attained" (see Phil. 3:12), I am overjoyed that in succeeding heart attacks (of which there have been three) the old enemy of fear has gradually been beaten down. In the most recent instance (1956), the feelings were as strong as during the first attack—that I was in my last moments, yet fear was totally absent. In spite of all my physical distress, I experienced a great peace. Faith, even the size of a mustard seed, can supplant any fear.

Spiritual Values

The Spirit is what gives life; the flesh does not help at all. The truths that I have told you are spirit and life (John 6:63).

Reshuffling my values is an uncomfortable yet delightful experience, often a pleasant surprise. Some things which for a long time I have assumed to be of first importance now appear less so. I wonder how I could have cherished them, held on to them, and sacrificed to secure them. For now I am discovering something of greater value—something vastly more important.

As I try to understand the mind of Christ, I see more and more clearly the supreme emphasis which he places on spiritual values and his indifference to the mad competition for money, power, honor, and prestige. Whatever Jesus touches he identifies with spiritual meaning. When he deals with a question, it is to relate it to eternal values. He never tarries in the forum of men's petty arguments but always lifts the discussion out into the broad realm of spiritual truth.

I hardly realize at first that my scale of values is undergoing a radical revision, so deftly does the change take place. But as I honestly try to acquire the outlook of the Master, yield my mind to the mind of Christ, I find that my viewpoints seem to change by themselves. I do not say to myself: "I must give up my old way of looking at this because I want to conform to what the Bible says, even if it is painful to do so." Rather, I experience a sort of awakening, a joyful realization that Jesus' emphasis or way of looking at a question, or his answer to some problem, is after all both sensible and satisfying.

Central to my new discoveries, and the one which is burning itself into my soul, is the realization that spiritual values constitute the basic reality. They alone will endure. All things will pass away; material achievements will disappear. Only the things of the spirit will ultimately remain. "So faith, hope, and love abide" (1 Cor. 13:13, RSV). These words of the great apostle reveal his grasp of the spirit of the Christ he served. Jesus' emphasis is on the spiritual aspect of any matter that comes to his attention. In some instances this is made evident by the *unimportance* which he attaches to the tangible and the temporal even more than by the positive worth. For example, when his disciples call his attention to the beautiful Temple at Jerusalem, he is not impressed by its magnificence but reminds them that it, too, will be destroyed (Luke 21:5-6).

More than ever before I am coming to understand what Paul means when he declares that a person becomes a new creature when he gets his thinking into line with the mind and spirit of Christ. "Old things are passed away; behold, all things are become new" (2 Cor. 5:17, KJV). A new attitude of mind can indeed transform one's entire life.

Heart Religion

For as he thinketh in his heart, so is he (Prov. 23:7a, KJV).

I have always been sensitive to sham in spiritual matters. I have tried as conscientiously as anyone to keep my life free of hypocrisy. Doubtless this attitude plays a part in my reorientation of religious values as the spiritual journey progresses. At any rate the quality of sincerity and genuineness in my religious life becomes for me the all-important consideration, almost to the point of obsession: the inner life, what I really am inside—my real self—is all that counts. Accordingly, I minimize the outward expressions of religious life. I become especially aware of the deadening effect of ceremonialism and ritual. I also reject whatever smacks of legalism in my search for answers to spiritual questions.

This firm position, which at times amounts almost to intolerance of formalism of any kind, really stems from the shock of that first crucial experience during and after my heart attack. In those moments of crisis, all the outward trappings of religion fall away. The only important consideration at that time is my personal relation to God. Doctrinal questions, the organized church, formal expressions of religion—all such matters are far out on the fringe. At the center is my real self, soon to meet God.

Later these conclusions are reinforced by months of reading and study. The main emphasis of Jesus also seems to bear out all my impressions. In his long conflict with the church authorities of his day, he consistently strives to free men from outward forms and direct them to the inner life. Always he stresses the "being" rather than the "doing." He frees people from slavery to the letter of the law and points them to the spirit. I begin to use the expression "heart religion" to identify Jesus' teaching, and the words appear more and more frequently in my notes.

Thus I am provided with a key for unlocking the Scriptures and am delighted with the spiritual vistas which it opens up to me. The studies which follow this chapter will, I hope, reflect this happy discovery. It is my intent that they shall reveal the emphasis which Jesus gives to life. The religion of the inner life, the union of the self with God, expresses for me the true essentials of religious experience.

Submission

Father, if you are willing, take this cup away from me. Yet not my will but always yours be done (Luke 22:42).

Not that I refer to any personal want, for I have learned to be contented with the circumstances that I am in. . . . I can do anything through Him who gives me strength (Phil. 4:11,13).

Few situations call for such radical readjustments as that facing the person who survives a heart attack. The very suddenness of it creates a crisis situation different from the accumulated resignation which filters gradually into the mind of one long accustomed to ill health.

I led an active life up to the very day. Then, all of a sudden, I face the stern demands of life under severe limitations. Oh yes, there had been the slowdown warning of the doctor some months before. I had discovered that I had angina, a hardening of the arteries. I entered the hospital for a checkup. They took my life history and gave me all the tests. Then they sent me home with solemn instructions to slow down and be careful. I have a talk with the dean and arrange for a slightly reduced schedule. I plan to rest a little every day. I am serious about the business, and think I have made a generous concession to life's demands. "After all, at my age . . . "

But the situation is not really urgent. Life goes on about as usual—until the sudden crisis. Then, of course, the picture is entirely different. I enter the convalescent period with a dull comprehension that though my life has been spared, my days of usefulness are over. I cannot bring myself to accept reality. There *must* be a way out. Life cannot do this to me! I have my work—I have just reached my greatest usefulness—I need at least ten years, I am counting on twenty. I will not accept it. I defy you to do that to me! Defy? Whom? Did I say, "I defy you?" *No, I cannot say that, I must not think that way. I know better than that, dear God, but what am I to do?*

So I come quickly to the realization that life *did* do that to me, and now it is my move. How am I going to meet it?

Here my old loyalties and years of Christian experience come to my rescue. Have I not built my life on God's infinite wisdom and mercy? "Who has ever known the Lord's thoughts, so that he can instruct Him?" (1 Cor. 2:16). Surely he will not leave me comfortless in my hour of need. Furthermore, it is folly to resist. The rigid wall confronts the hurricane and is blown down, while the tree bends to the storm and the winds pass over it. Nature's way is best. I am able, therefore, after the first panic of rebellion, to throw myself on God's mercy and yield my will to his in faith. It is true submission. The first great commitment brings peace to my troubled soul.

I discover that it is one thing to submit, by act of will, and something else again to *carry out a program* of submission. Without hesitation I say that true submission to God's will is the first and greatest essential in adjusting one's life to adversity and disappointment. But with equal emphasis I warn against the wrong conception of submission. Submission does not mean an inert resignation to fate, a passive acceptance of misfortune and disaster. Holy submission to the will of our Heavenly Father is something virile and active, yes, something determinedly aggressive. Dull fatalism does not describe the life of him who is the most submissive one of all time, the Lord Jesus Christ. His greatest hour of submission—in Gethsemane—is followed by the most positive and far-reaching act of history. In his submission to the Father, Jesus is cooperating with God to carry out the will of God.

In the sense of cooperating with God, submission fits the forefront of any formula for overcoming hard circumstances. Thus, submission is not surrender, but victory. It does not cancel out the idea of "never give up" or the personal factors of courage and determination. Rather, submission to God transcends those human factors and gathers them up *in coalition with a great Ally of strength*, an Ally who takes control and directs the campaign.

I do not fully appreciate this for some time. I spend many hours in useless anxiety lest my total surrender to God's will might actually hinder my recovery by acting as a roadblock to that important attitude of grit and determination. I come to realize, however, that in yielding to God's will I am really "latching on" to great power and making it possible for me to cooperate with him in appropriating and using that power. I discover Paul's great secret in this matter (a "secret," however, which he loudly proclaims) when he tells the Philippian Christians that he has learned to be content in any circumstance. In the very next breath he adds that the secret lies in the fact that he *can do anything* through Christ who gives him strength. His submission is full of humility, but it is geared to tremendous power, and Paul uses that power.

The Attitude of Gratitude

Continue giving thanks for everything to God our Father (Eph. 5:20).

The first rule for overcoming a serious handicap is this: never feel sorry for yourself. The corollary: count your blessings. Self-pity is defeatism. The false self must be submerged, not pampered, if one is to regain health, either physical or mental.

When I awaken from my night's rest and say, "Thank you, God, for the privilege of life," it is more than merely the thought of "lucky me." My attitude is inclusive—embracing the entire concept of submission, trust, spiritual reality, hope, and love. I thank the Heavenly Father for everything in a spontaneous feeling of joy in partnership with him. That particular enemy, self-pity, may be lurking in the shadows but I am hardly aware of it. Instead of being called out for open combat, self-pity is smothered under the total impact of the attitude of gratitude. To be in union with Christ is to be a new creature— *all* things have become new as I look at life, including the impulse to give thanks and the kindred feeling to be glad rather than sorry for myself.

My new attitude of mind is rooted in a deep personal commitment to Christ from a basic sense of trust. My dependence on God, strengthened by a continuing spiritual experience, makes it easy and natural for me to feel thankful regardless of circumstances. My new experience has extended from months into years, surviving repeated setbacks—hospitalizations, convalescences, and dashed hopes for more complete recovery.

In spite of all these high-sounding affirmations, I must confess that I have more than once been obliged to fall back on the simple rules. Like all believers I have found that spiritual health is not constant, but that we have many ups and downs. In the drab and commonplace hours I have had to brace my morale against that last-ditch support and say, "Count your blessings and be glad you can count." Then I call to mind the many who are less fortunate than I, and for the time hope to beat down the adversary. For, let it be known that this battle is not won once and for all but must be waged again and again. Each victory over self-pity adds to the cumulative strength of one's morale. And the spiritual journey does not always follow the valleys. The highlands give stability, while at intervals from inspiration points we regain perspective.

Creative Crises

In such a hope keep on rejoicing, although for a little while you must be sorrow-stricken with various trials, so that the genuineness of your faith, which is more precious than gold that perishes even after it is shown by the test of fire to be genuine, may result in your praise and glory and honor at the unveiling of Jesus Christ. You must continue to love Him, although you have never seen Him, but because you do believe in Him, although you do not now see Him, you must continue to rejoice with an unutterable and triumphant joy (1 Pet. 1:6-8).

And not only that, but this too: let us continue exulting in our
sufferings, for we know that suffering produces endurance, and
endurance, tested character, and tested character, hope, and hope
never disappoints us; for through the Holy Spirit that has been given
us, God's love has flooded our hearts (Rom. 5:3-5).

How to deal with trouble is my problem all along. The
answers are beginning to unfold, but so much yet remains
obscure. I recall something in the Bible about tribulation
working patience—but who wants to be patient? I am growing
impatient; moreover I do not want to look up that verse. I want
to do something positive and constructive about the problem.
Yet it is all there in "that verse" could I but face it—how
adversity actually enriches life through a deeper understanding
of God's laws and their working out in human experience.
What can be more active and vigorous, more creative, than the
struggle for character and spiritual growth?

We glibly say that a person has not lived who has not
suffered. I can go along with that, provided the person has
made some effort to understand the meaning of suffering.
Trials and tribulations are not necessarily enriching experiences
in themselves. It all depends on one's response. Trouble may
leave one person soured and embittered, while another becomes kind in spirit and stronger in character. It may be
destructive or it may be creative. What makes the difference?

For years I was aware of a body of Christian literature
dealing with pain, suffering, and other forms of distress. I had
never bothered to read any of these writings. I suppose I
thought they were for unfortunate folk who needed some
mental aspirin to relieve their bruised spirits. Now I too was in
serious need, and for something more than a palliative. If there
was an answer to the problem of suffering, particularly of
disappointments and broken hopes, I wanted to find it. I
wanted a positive answer which would provide an incentive to

push on and not give up. Surely there must be help in the Bible.

I began where thousands of others have doubtless gone—in the Book of Job. I note the shock of sudden misfortune, the doubt and fear, the utter frustration. Out of it comes an early note of triumphant faith rising from the depths of despair. But it does not suffice for me, as it did not for Job. My search is not fruitless, but a full answer still eludes me. I go to the New Testament for that.

The problem of suffering in its deeper, positive meaning appears only with the complete revelation in Christ. Looking at his life and death, I begin to understand the strange truth that God's ways are mostly paradoxical. I learn to "fly by instrument" rather than trust my faulty vision, and the craft becomes steady. I find that misfortune may be a blessing in disguise, that the greatest joy comes through pain, that strength is found in weakness, and simple faith confounds the wisdom of men. Gradually I sense what is perhaps the greatest paradox of all, that suffering is the price of all that is good—a truth encompassed in the meaning of the cross itself. I realize that suffering—pain, adversity, trials, disappointments—not only may be a constructive experience for one, but that it is God's most creative agent in a world still controlled by his infinite wisdom.

As these insights dawn in my thinking, life takes on deeper meaning and purpose. It is entirely an inner experience but it changes my outlook. It is a paradox in itself, for while I have less to live for in terms of personal satisfaction and professional prospects, I am experiencing the greatest incentive to live and the greatest joy of living that I have ever known.

2
The Kingdom of God

Life's Fulfillment

Do not suppose that I have come to set aside the law or the prophets. I have not come to set them aside but to fill them up to the brim (Matt. 5:17-18a).

In his emphasis on the inner life, Jesus has to take a stand concerning the legalistic system which has preempted the place of true religion in Israel. He is determined to break through and lead the way to something better. The "something" is the key to the situation. Jesus' clash with the religious leaders does not stem from a desire to destroy. His program is a positive one, his gospel is a fulfillment. But it is not meant to fulfill the deadly minutiae of tradition. The blanket of legalism which covered the religious life of the time would smother the free and joyous spirit which Jesus is releasing among people. Such a spirit cannot be contained within the restraining confines of ceremonial forms and legalistic minds.

No, it is not the "joy of battle" that drives Jesus into the continuing flight with formalism. It is the *joy of life* filled to overflowing with God's spirit. He finds himself in an environment of religious observances which act as a straightjacket to his sensitive nature. The result: *his spirit breaks for freedom.*

Jesus does not propose to uproot the law of Moses. His own faith is rooted deep in his Hebrew heritage. He draws inspiration from the great spiritual insights of the Old Testament. So he starts with the law, but he does not intend to stop with it. His goal is the kingdom of heaven. While the law must indeed be observed, it cannot be observed as the scribes and Pharisees observe it.

What then does Jesus mean by insisting that the law must be observed, when in the same breath he condemns those who are most scrupulous in its observance? In the Sermon on the Mount he makes it clear that when people keep the Law as it *should* be kept, and as God intends it to be kept, they experience the kingdom of heaven. Jesus is telling us that God intends for us to observe the forms of religion in spirit, not as ends. The kingdom of heaven is the law made spiritual, transplanted from the soil of external forms to that of the inner life. To be in the kingdom of heaven is to shift the emphasis from the outward act to inner desire, from doing to being. Jesus, therefore, fulfills the law by completing it and giving it rich new meaning.

All that Jesus says about the Jewish law applies in full measure to every outward observance of religion today. This realization helped me resolve some of the frustrations which were present at the start of this spiritual journey. I have stated that the "trappings" of religion had fallen away, and if I said it rather contemptuously I was only recording my true feelings in those tense days. The church itself—its doctrinal disputations, its multifarious meetings, its "religiosity"—all were minimized in a fierce determination to recognize only the essentials. But one of the most helpful ways to gain perspective is to go on a journey. I am finding this true in a spiritual sense.

Intrinsic Worth

And how much more a man is worth than a sheep! So, it is right to do good on the Sabbath (Matt. 12:12).

When the Jewish leaders challenge Jesus for breaking the sabbath law, he refuses to admit that God's displeasure rests on a technicality. He asserts boldly that he, the Son of Man, is Master of the sabbath. He is telling them that people must prevail over the insidious snares of legalistic religion. He is insisting again that God is not pleased with mere form, that nothing counts unless it comes from the heart. With Jesus, one's real self, his attitudes and motives, are everything. Merely to go through the motions, whether it be in some burdensome trivia or even in a meaningful and beautiful ritual, is all emptiness if one's heart is not in it.

So sharp is this issue of sabbath observance that it produces one of the most intense clashes of Jesus' ministry, and occasions the display of daring courage as he meets his enemies in a head-on collision. They bring a man with a crippled hand to the synagogue on the sabbath day and place him where Jesus will have to pass by. They dare him to heal the man on the sabbath day. The issue is clearly drawn. The Pharisees put the question themselves: "Is it right to cure people on the Sabbath?" (v. 10). We wonder how anyone could seriously ask such a question. But the fact that they could and did reveals what the curse of legalism can do to people's minds. Reminding them that they will lift a sheep out of a hole on the sabbath, Jesus exclaims, "How much more a man is worth than a sheep!"

The worth of a person—that is the touchstone which Jesus uses for evaluating religion. Does it minister to people's need? Away with rules which keep one from doing good on the sabbath! Mark says that Jesus looks around at them with anger, hurt by their obstinacy. After he has healed the man, those who engineered the plan are "filled with fury" (Luke 6:11). But Jesus is equally determined. He is determined that God shall not be imprisoned in a system of religious restraints.

A Loyalty Test

Go, sell everything you have, and give the money to the poor, and you will have riches in heaven; then come back and follow me (Mark 10:21b).

When the young man comes to Jesus asking how to make sure his salvation, he runs head-on into a concept of goodness which is new to him: that goodness and eternal life are matters of character dependent on one's inner life rather than outward works or keeping the Commandments. He learns that there is a plane of spiritual living higher than a good moral life. The point of this incident about the "rich young ruler" is not merely that riches keep one out of the kingdom of God but that entrance into the kingdom is dependent upon the deep desire of one's heart. It is a matter of loyalty. When wealth and riches claim our first allegiance, they *automatically* cut us off from God and his kingdom.

In answer to the young man's query on how to be assured of eternal life, Jesus first points to the Commandments, specifically naming several. It is significant that he does not include any concerning Jewish ritual or altar worship, nothing at all of ceremonial nature. All deal with morality and ethics, or with one's relation to others. The applicant easily passes this first test for admission into the kingdom.

Then Jesus gives him a second one. It is essentially a loyalty test. Jesus knows that where one's treasure is, there will the heart be—one's real allegiance. He sees that money and things had become first in the life of this young man. His *attitude* toward money, rather than the wealth itself, keeps him out of the kingdom of God. When he fails to pass this test, Jesus is saddened because nothing Jesus can do now will bring the young man into the kingdom of God.

The incident reminds us that we keep ourselves out of the full experience of God by the scale of values which we set up in our deep inner consciousness. We rationalize about security and standards of living. Soon those standards are all mixed up with ease and luxury. Eventually money and things come to be what we most desire deep down in our hearts. Spiritual values are dethroned for material values. No wonder Jesus is led to remark on how hard it is for those who have wealth to enter the kingdom of God.

Heart Care

Be ever on the alert and always on your guard against every form of greed (Luke 12:15a).

For wherever your treasure is, there too your heart will be (Matt. 6:21).

A man comes to Jesus with the request that Jesus intercede for him in securing the rightful share of his inheritance. But Jesus refuses to arrogate to himself the duties of a probate judge. Here is a man who perhaps is being robbed of his rightful inheritance, yet to Jesus this possible injustice is no assurance against greed entering the man's own heart and eating away his character. "Man, who made me a judge or an umpire of your affairs?" he asked, and then quickly added:

"Be ever on the alert and always on your guard against every form of greed." A fair settlement of the estate, laudable as that may be, is not the real issue in Jesus' mind. The big thing is the man's attitude toward the money he so much wants. The question calls forth a parable from Jesus about a man who is indeed rich in money but is not "rich in God" (v. 21). It is bound to be either God or mammon, he says. One of them will win out in a person's life. Both cannot be first, for they are in constant conflict.

Jesus does not condemn wealth as such. He is so greatly concerned about the vicious influence it has on people that he simply avoids it like poison. He neither condemns the making of money honestly, nor does he condemn the right use of money. But he pleads with people to keep it in its rightful place, and that place is far, far below the things of the spirit. He is himself so utterly indifferent to wealth, so unconcerned about his own material needs, so unimpressed by the presence of the rich or the power which their riches give them, that his attitude is almost one of contempt. If we view Jesus honestly, freed from our preconceptions about him, we find his position on money baffling to our twentieth-century minds. Some of our most respected ideas (about thrift or security, for example) do not find in Jesus' teachings the full sanctity with which they are clothed in Christian circles today.

On numerous occasions Jesus calls attention to the fact that the pleasure of being rich crowds out the spiritual word. Riches stand between the young ruler of the synagogue and the abundant life. The loss of their hogs, incident to the healing of the demoniac, led the people of Gerasa to demand the departure of the very Son of God (see Mark 5). In the parable of the sower, the "cares of the world, and the delight in riches" (Mark 4:19, RSV) are the thorns which choke the Word. We should not be surprised that he forbids his own disciples to take money or travel accessories on their missionary journeys. One who is effective in spiritual matters is unencumbered by material interests.

Built-in Altruism

Let us go somewhere else, to the neighboring towns, to preach in them, too, for that is why I came out here (Mark 1:38).

The early chapters of Mark's Gospel present scenes alive with action. In the center of it is Jesus, emerging from an inconspicuous background among lowly people. His rise to fame is immediate. In a few short months he becomes the center of attention on the part of thousands. The crowds throng about him. People come from all over Galilee, from Judea, and Jerusalem, from across the Jordan, even from Tyre and Sidon. Why do they flock to him? One obvious reason is his healing activity. "He told His disciples to keep a little boat ready for Him all the time to prevent the crowds from crushing Him. For He cured so many people that all who had ailments kept crowding up against Him to touch Him" (Mark 3:9-10).

But people also come to listen to his message. It is arresting, fresh, and different, and he speaks with authority—his words carry conviction. He impresses his hearers as one who knows what he is talking about. They listen attentively, they hang on his words, they follow him about the country that they might hear more.

No tricks of eloquence induce people to listen to Jesus. He is speaking to them of matters which touch their lives vitally. He talks about a way of life that brings peace and happiness. He tells them he comes to give them abundant life. Above all, he speaks out of his own experience. He is experiencing God in his life. It is something so wonderful, so satisfying, so unspeakably joyful, that he is driven to tell how it can be had. His life is dominated by this urge to share his experience. He *must* share it with others; in fact, *the need to share it is part of it.* He cannot live quietly to himself and remain true to himself.

When we read the message, we see Jesus himself. His words and ideas are an extension of his own personality. His teachings constitute a record of his own experience with God and with people. He is able to impart abundant life because his own life is so abundantly filled with God. He knows a great joy of living. He is free from worry and anxiety; his Heavenly Father is real to him, as real as the people around him. Between him and God there is a deep and rich fellowship. These experiences he tries to pass on to others; he has a compelling urge to do so.

In view of all this, the question comes: Have I even yet discovered the kingdom of God? Am I experiencing the abundant life which Jesus knew and do I feel a similar urgency to pass it on to others? If the need to share it is part of it, then a Christian cannot live to himself. One must share it in order to experience it. One receives as one gives.

Their Reward

So whenever you do your deeds of charity, never blow your own horn in public, as the hypocrites are in the habit of doing in the synagogues and the street corners, to be praised by people. I solemnly say to you, they already have their reward (Matt. 6:2).

One of the most poignant phrases in the New Testament is the expression used by Jesus concerning those whose motives are selfish in their almsgiving and prayer. "They already have their reward," says Jesus.

What is their reward? It is the public praise. Some must feel that praise is indeed a reward worth striving for, to judge by the effort that people put forth to win it. And Jesus is content to let them have it. He seems to say: "That's what they wanted, they paid the price for it, let them enjoy it."

To Jesus that is tragic. For us to accept the tawdry substitute of praise, which may inflate our ego but devastate our character, while rejecting the genuine thing—God's approval—is indeed a lamentable choice. Thus Jesus probes our hearts. Always he reaches back to our motives, our honesty, our ultimate purpose. We are measured by his ultimate purpose which is to glorify the Father.

Especially in prayer is it important to be sincere. When you pray, says Jesus, pray in secret, and "you must not keep on repeating empty phrases" (v. 7). That expression grips our attention. Think of the thousands of empty phrases that clutter up our daily lives—trivial talk, superfluous verbiage, double-talk, deceptive speech. In some situations empty phrases are even considered good. They are useful for making conversation, helpful in smoothing over the rough terrain that separates our minds and personalities one from the other. Perhaps in human relations there is a place for small talk. But when we talk to God we do not need it. Empty phrases simply do not reach him. They evaporate as soon as we utter them. Only the real gets through to God. Only what is genuine and honest can possibly reach the heart of God, because God is truth itself, God is the essence of honesty.

Self-revelation

Beware of the yeast of the Pharisees, that is, hypocrisy. There is
nothing covered up that will not be uncovered, nor secret that will not
be made known (Luke 12:2).

As I study the Gospel writings, I become more and more
impressed with Jesus' demands for character. Honesty, sincerity, truth—the qualities which we think of as plain decency
and integrity—are basic with Jesus. Shame and pretense
simply cannot be tolerated. The inside of the cup must be
clean. Keeping the letter of the law of Moses ever so scru-
pulously while neglecting the moral precepts draws from Jesus
a blast of indignant protest and condemnation. Justice and
love must come first before ritual. They are the root of
character. Of all the things which destroy character, hypocrisy
is one of the worst. It is a dangerous poison, a most insidious
thing which grows like yeast. Jesus speaks of it that way, calling
it the leaven of the Pharisees.

Then he adds this significant warning: "There is nothing
covered up that will not be uncovered, nor secret that will not
be made known; because what you have spoken in darkness
will be heard in the light, and what you whispered in people's
ears, behind closed doors, will be proclaimed from the house-
tops" (vv. 2-3). In other words, hypocrisy is of no avail
whatever in achieving the purpose to which it is put. One's true
character will be known by everybody, like what is seen in
broad daylight or shouted from the housetop. *Hypocrisy, used
for purpose of deceit, merely serves as a window to reveal
one's true self.* Thus it defeats itself. But alas, its effect on a
person's character is disastrous, and Jesus considers it to be a
tragic thing.

Why is character of supreme importance? Jesus proceeds to

tell why in this same passage: because of one's worth in the eyes of God. Even the sparrows are worth something in God's sight, but as for a person, the very hairs of one's head are counted! "You are worth more than many sparrows" (v. 7). What a tremendous thought! Everyone is worth something, even the most lowly. The most abased person in the world has intrinsic value. Jesus emphasizes it over and over by word and deed. When released in the world, this idea produces revolutions and remakes society. Is it any wonder that the gospel of Christ is a message of hope?

Inward Proof

Only a wicked and treacherous age is hankering for a spectacular sign, and no sign will be given it but the sign of the prophet Jonah (Matt. 12:39).

Jesus does not value his gospel lightly. He is convinced that it is supremely valuable. He is gripped by his own message. He is hurt when people in their waywardness refuse to give ear to the truths which to him are self-evident. When, in the face of all this, they demand a sign, some outward proof of his right to speak, he is exasperated with them. No sign will be given them, he says, except the sign of Jonah. Then, perhaps mindful of his recent preaching, he declares that, whereas the men of Nineveh repented when Jonah preached to them, "There is more than Jonah here!" Furthermore, the queen of the south came from afar to listen to Solomon's wisdom, but "there is more than Solomon here!"

He is saying to them: *I* am here, I with my message, my gospel, my way of life. Jonah and Solomon are not to be compared with the boon which God is bestowing upon mankind in the sending of his Son. Why, then, should there be need for any evidence of Jesus' sonship other than the marvelous words of life which he declares and his yet more marvelous life? No sensational proof is considered necessary by him. Any kind of spectacular demonstration would be superfluous. No, Jesus can see no need for a "spectacular" sign; he will not throw himself from a temple tower. He is his own set of credentials. His life of love and joy is more compelling than any outward manifestation. He is much more than a Jonah or a Solomon. He is to be accepted in faith and experienced in the richness of the life he gives.

Is it not a fair question to ask whether we are demanding that Jesus give us a sign before we fully believe in him? We ask it in the sense that we desire some tangible proof that his gospel will really work before we accept his help, that is, fully depend on him. We want to see some spectacular evidence of his power before launching out "on faith." We would like to experience the reality of his presence in our lives, but we are not ready to meet the conditions for it. "Let it happen to me, and then I'll believe it," we say.

Unconsciously perhaps, we are asking for a trial demonstration before we buy. But Jesus does not fit into that pattern. The only way we can "try out" his gospel is to accept it for keeps. It comes free but not in a free trial package. Tentative acceptance of Christ is nonacceptance because only by a full surrender can we enter into the kingdom. Paul reminded the Christians of Rome that "a hope that is seen is not real hope, for who hopes for what he actually sees?" (Rom. 8:25). Likewise, a relationship based on faith, such as our relation to Christ, can be real only as we walk in faith and refrain from asking for exceptional manifestations.

3
Exploring the Kingdom of God

Without Boundaries

What is the kingdom of God like? To what may I compare it? (Luke 13:18a).

One does not travel far on a journey through the Gospel narratives before entering a wonderful new country without boundaries known as the kingdom of God. For me, one of the major features of this spiritual journey is the rediscovery of the kingdom of God.

My interest is focused particularly on the personal aspect of this inclusive concept. An entirely new meaning is emerging. Instead of the social dimensions of the kingdom which largely fashioned my thinking previously, I am seeing the kingdom of God as a pattern for my personal life, involving my inner attitudes as well as my outward acts and including every area of my life. In one sense this is not new, however. What is new is that I have discovered its real source, the life of the Master himself. Jesus was the kingdom of God. The term has come to signify for me an experience of God like that which Jesus is having in his own life as he launches the new movement which he calls the kingdom of God.

Jesus talks about the kingdom with unbounded enthusiasm. But he has difficulty in getting people to understand it and experience it as he does. He realizes that this new way which he has found and wants to share is too profound for a simple explanation. It is an experience which encompasses all of life. The kingdom of God has more than one set of dimensions; it cannot fit into a single frame of reference. Therefore Jesus presents it from various angles, holding it up as one might exhibit a precious jewel, viewing it from first one side and then another. The kingdom of God, he says, is comparable to the sowing of seed, it is like the mustard seed itself, or the yeast in bread. Again, it is like a hidden treasure, a costly pearl. In other ways, the kingdom of God can be compared to a great dinner party, or it is like a net that is let down in the sea and encloses fish of all kinds.

And so the Master uses word pictures, one after another, each presenting some aspect of the kingdom. But while the parables bring out various elements in it, one is common to nearly all of them, namely the element of personal experience and responsibility. Jesus' personal relation with his Heavenly Father is at the heart of his own experience and thus a central feature of the kingdom of God. Jesus draws the pattern for it out of his own life. As he looks into his inner self, he finds there the true principles of life. No wonder that he considers it the most-to-be-desired experience in the world.

To one taking a spiritual pilgrimage it is a wonderful new country awaiting discovery. What a challenge to go in and explore it!

Like Unto a Priceless Pearl

Again, the kingdom of heaven is like a gem-dealer who was looking for beautiful pearls. One day he found a very costly pearl, and went and sold all he had, and bought it (Matt. 13:45-46).

To Jesus the kingdom of heaven is supremely important; it is desirable above all else. He tries to get his followers to see it that way and feel that way about it. It is a pearl of great price, a treasure of tremendous value, the possession of which gives ultimate satisfaction and happiness. The merchant in the parable sacrifices everything he has in order to obtain the one thing of supreme worth.

Even in paying tribute to John the Baptist, Jesus reveals the high value he places on the kingdom of God. There is no greater person than John, he says as a climax to an appreciative eulogy. Then, as if bringing himself back to the realities of the new order which John initiated and which he, Jesus, is carrying to completion, he adds: "Yet he who is least in the kingdom of God is greater than he" (Luke 7:28, RSV).

That is how important the kingdom of God is to Jesus. If John, the greatest of the prophets, is less than the least in the kingdom of God, what a privilege it is to enter this kingdom! John comes close to it; he reveals true spiritual insight in his demand for repentance and inner spiritual quality. But the kingdom of God goes beyond John's experience. Jesus not only preached the kingdom of God, he lived it.

So when Jesus likened his way of life to a priceless possession, he was saying that it has the value of life itself. How could he have presented it more forcibly? Surely it deserves our attention. It is worth knowing about; it is worth trying. As the Christian experiences the kingdom of God in his own life, he verifies all that Jesus says about this matchless pearl.

Invitation, RSVP

For I tell you, not one of those people who were invited shall get a taste of my dinner! (Luke 14:24).

A guest at the table remarks on how wonderful it will be at

the banquet in the kingdom of God. In reply, Jesus tells a story about a man who gives a great dinner, but the invited guests begin sending their regrets. They are detained for various reasons, and (contrary to the accepted view) I consider them good, reasonable excuses. They are not trivial alibis but urgent matters of business and family affairs. Surely one must look after his business, and who would ask a man to abandon his bride during the honeymoon?

But the point of the story is that the invited guests failed to realize that this invitation is more important even than any of these matters. They do not mean to ignore the invitation, but they feel that other interests should come first. These other matters, whether they appear trivial or important, are more important in the lives of the people involved than the dinner to which they are invited. So they give these matters first attention by choice. They *do not desire* the banquet experience as much. Thus Jesus teaches that the kingdom of God must be desired above all other desires if we would enter it. Desire is the key.

I wonder, however, if our lack of desire does not stem from the fact that we are not fully aware of what the kingdom of God really is and can do for us. It is not something that we do for ourselves, but something done *to* us. The apostle Paul says that it makes us new creatures, so that everything is seen in a new light. That which was formerly important to us recedes to the background, while new values crowd to the front.

Christ's way does not come easy. We must make an effort to attain it. Jesus follows up this parable with an exhortation on counting the cost before accepting discipleship with him. "Whoever does not persevere in carrying his own cross and thus following after me, cannot be a disciple of mine" (v. 27), he says. Quality always comes high. Most of us are unwilling to buy; we think we cannot afford it. We concede that Jesus is right, but we remain attached to lesser values. Too often we send our regrets.

New and Revolutionary

For the kingdom of heaven is like an owner of an estate who went out early in the morning to hire laborers for his vineyard (Matt. 20:1).

Jesus compares the kingdom of God to the inaugurating of a brand-new wage system. The employer goes out early in the morning to hire workmen. He makes an agreement with them as to their wages, and at day's end he pays them as he has promised. But meanwhile he hires others at different hours of the day, hence they do not give a full day's work. But this employer does an odd thing; he pays everyone alike. Naturally a protest goes up from the group who has toiled all day from the early hours through the midday heat. But the employer insists that he has kept his agreement with them and that he has the right to do as he pleases with his own money. "Do you begrudge my generosity?" (v. 15, RSV), he asks.

For many years, when I would read this story, my sympathy was with the men who put in a full day's work and yet were forced to see others who had worked only a fraction of the time step up and receive the same reward as they. It violated my sense of justice and I secretly felt that Jesus might have made his point in some more effective way. The truth is that I had missed the point myself.

What is the point which Jesus wishes to make? He states it at the very beginning and clinches it at the end. "The kingdom of heaven is like . . . , " he begins. Then he weaves a story which sounds unusual to us, accustomed as we are to measure everything in terms of service rendered and value received.

But herein lies the main point. The kingdom of heaven is *not* like the daily relationships of men, economic or otherwise. Spiritual matters are not subject to the kind of measurement with which we estimate the value of labor or the cost of management. In the kingdom of heaven there is no place for time sheets and payrolls. The things of the spirit are not to be broken down into periods of tenure, priority, or time segments of any sort. God's children are all on an equality before him; *all* may receive the full measure of his spiritual blessing.

Moreover, the rewards in the kingdom of heaven are given, not earned. A key word in the story is the word *generosity*. "Do you begrudge my generosity?" asks the owner of the vineyard. God's dealings with men are not on the basis of anything earned or merited. It is only through his generous and forgiving love that we may enjoy fellowship with him. "So," said Christ, "those who are last now will be first then, and those first will be last" (v. 16), which is to say that there isn't any such thing as first ones and last ones around the throne of God. Our prevailing scale of values is worthless in the kingdom of heaven. We may as well try to measure outer space in bushel baskets as to apply ordinary commercial values to spiritual reality.

> For the love of God is broader
> Than the measure of man's mind;
> And the heart of the eternal
> Is most wonderfully kind.

FREDERICK W. FABER

How fathomless the depths of God's resources, wisdom, and knowledge! How unsearchable His decisions, and how mysterious His methods! For who has ever understood the thoughts of the Lord, or has ever been His adviser? Or who has ever advanced God anything to have Him pay him back? For from

Him everything comes, through Him everything lives, and for Him everything exists. Glory to Him forever! Amen (Rom. 11:33-36).

As We Forgive Our Debtors

So the kingdom of heaven may be compared to a king who decided to settle up his accounts with his slaves (Matt. 18:23).

When Peter comes to Jesus asking about the matter of forgiveness, he is told that there is no limit to the spirit of forgiveness. That is the nature of forgiveness; it is without limits. If we start out to keep books, whether stopping at seven or seventy times seven, we haven't really forgiven at all. What is more, we have failed in an important respect to qualify for the kingdom of heaven.

It is characteristic of Jesus to follow up his words on forgiveness with a parable about the kingdom of heaven. The kingdom of heaven is the frame of reference for his thinking about spiritual matters. It represents the area of life where such spiritual effort as forgiveness takes place. The kingdom of heaven is the objective toward which he expects us, as he expected Peter, to strive. "So," says Jesus, "the kingdom of heaven may be compared to" a situation involving forgiveness.

The story which follows sets forth in striking contrast the enormity of the debt which a king forgives his servant and the trifling sum which the servant refuses to forgive his debtor. The story moves along to a perfectly logical conclusion: the unforgiving servant is punished for his failure to forgive as he has been forgiven. Finally the application, concisely stated: "This is the way my heavenly Father will deal with you, if you do not, each one, heartily forgive your brother" (v. 35).

Could it be otherwise? What earthly king could overlook such heartless ingratitude on the part of a subject? Such a king would be unworthy of the royal name! Then how logical it is that God must deal likewise with us according to similar conditions. Is not God's universe organized on that basis? If we refuse to forgive, can we really accept God's forgiveness? To be unforgiving is to be self-condemned. We make it impossible for God's forgiveness to reach us. The parable shows that the unforgiving servant simply cannot remain a forgiven servant.

Within the kingdom of God there are laws of the realm. Of these spiritual laws, that of forgiveness is one of the most important. Its influence on the one who forgives is even greater than on the one forgiven. When the spirit of forgiveness goes out of the heart, it leaves a vacuum which is filled at once with resentment and hate, the enemies of forgiveness. The poison thus produced soon infects other areas of the inner life and one's whole character is in danger of deterioration. But a forgiving spirit has the opposite effect. It acts as a wonder drug to destroy the enemies of character. It serves to qualify one for the kingdom of heaven.

Like Unto a Humble Heart

Two men went up to the temple to pray, one a Pharisee, the other a tax-collector (Luke 18:10).

The story method cannot be surpassed for the purpose of teaching truth. Jesus' use of the parable is superb; he is a master storyteller. His pedagogy is perfect in selecting material and making it serve his purpose.

The petitions of the two men who went to the temple to pray, as presented in contrast to each other, reveal more of

Christ's message than could be given in many pages of learned discourse. The Pharisee congratulates himself because he pays his tithe and fasts according to the law—he observes the forms of religion. But the publican has faced his real self. He is repentant. He knows that he needs God's mercy. On the one hand is pride, on the other, humility. On the one hand is self-deception, on the other, self-encounter. Jesus says the humble person receives God's approval.

More subtle distinctions are also involved in the story. Why was this publican so distressed over his own condition? Was it because he failed to keep the law, to pay tithes and fast? No, his kind of repentance comes from more grievous sins. He knows he has sinned, not merely omitted a rite. He confesses his sin to God. His is a contrite heart.

The Pharisee, on the other hand, is free from those black sins which the publican is probably confessing. Greed, dishonesty, and adultery are not among the sins of the Pharisee, according to his own affidavit to God. Those are sins which Jesus also condemns along with the outward forms of legalism. Yet this man does not win God's approval by his ethics, his purity of life, or a heart free from greed any more than by his strict observance of the law. What, then, is his trouble? Jesus gives the key when he introduces the Pharisee as one who "prayed thus with himself" (v. 11, RSV). Thus the matchless storyteller reveals at the start the basic problem: a proud heart. The Pharisee, with such an attitude, cannot pray to God. He can only pray "with himself." His good life is not enough; it lacks the contrite heart.

From this meditation we learn the value and the place of a humble and contrite heart. This quality is needed as we pray for forgiveness and as we seek to find God's help in the crises of life. Our goodness is not sufficient; only God can see us through the valley.

Like Unto Humble Service

Then He poured water into a basin and began to wash the disciples'
feet (John 13:5a).

Perhaps the quality most needed but all too rare among
Christians today is a humble spirit. How often does Jesus
emphasize it! And how forcefully he tries to drive it home to his
disciples! What quality was more frequently exemplified in his
own life than that of humility? Having taught it repeatedly by
word and example in his association with the twelve, he
crowns this aspect of his ministry at their last meeting in the
upper room. Taking towel and basin, he washes his disciples'
feet, a service ordinarily performed by a servant. Then he says
to them: "If I then, your Lord and Teacher, have washed your
feet, you also ought to wash one another's feet too. For I have
set you an example" (vv. 14-15). With this impressive demonstration and these explicit instructions, Jesus seeks to make the
spirit of humility a vital part of his legacy. He wants it to sink
deep into the consciousness of those to whom he is entrusting
his message.

Only one of the four Gospel writers was inspired to include
the incident in the account of that memorable last supper. John
gives us a full account, even to the significant introductory
statement in verse 3: "Jesus, . . . sure that the Father had put
everything into His hands, and that He had come from God
and was going back to God, got up from the table, took off His
outer clothing, and took a towel and tied it around His waist"
(vv. 2-4). Why was John inspired to make the comment if not
to remind us that humility comes easy to those who are aware
of God's approval of themselves and who feel no need of
popular esteem? Pride and arrogance betoken a desire for the
deference and admiration of others. Such a spirit is born of a

self-centered life; it exhibits weakness and frustration. Humility, on the other hand, issues from serenity, from a composure based on the assurance of God's favor because one is doing his will. That person *can afford* to be humble. But humility is a luxury which the proud must forego; they lack the relationship by which it can be obtained.

Like Unto a Little Child

Just at that moment the disciples came up and asked Jesus, "Who then is greatest in the kingdom of heaven?" (Matt. 18:1).

The disciples came asking Jesus who is greatest in the kingdom of heaven. It is such a natural thing to ask, that is, such a human thing. We tend to think of people by categories. We evaluate and compare. We must identify the "big wheels" and the lesser ones. Our world is like that.

But Jesus' conception is entirely different. Nothing else marks him off from ordinary men so sharply as this matter of greatness. The disciples wanted to know who is the greatest. Why should there be any need for a "greatest" in this kingdom of God which Jesus is proclaiming? He envisions a community of persons whose lives are motivated to serve, not to be served, people seeking no special honor or distinction. His scale of values here is diametrically opposite to mankind's age-long practice. "Whoever wants to be great among you," he says, "must be your servant . . . your slave" (20:26-27).

In actual truth this is probably the most poorly practiced of all Jesus' teachings. Rare is the leader even among Christ's followers who approaches the Master's criterion of greatness. The gulf between the human passion for prestige, recognition, and power on the one hand and the model of Jesus on the other is so wide that there are few who come near to bridging it. Jesus succeeds because the desire to serve stems from deep wells of love. His attitudes and his passion for service determine his scale of values. Personal glory has no place there. Only the Father in heaven is to be glorified.

When he seeks to impart his view to the disciples, he takes a child and sets him in their midst, saying: "Unless you turn and become like little children, you can never get into the kingdom of heaven at all" (v. 3). Will they grasp his meaning and share his spirit? Shortly thereafter he said to the sons of Zebedee, when their mother had sought preferred positions for them: "You do not realize what you are asking for" (20:22). How true that was, and is. There is a vast gulf between God's criteria for life and our own self-centered values.

Like Unto a Mystery

"The kingdom of God," he said, "is like a man who scatters seed on the ground, and then continues sleeping by night and getting up by day, while the seed sprouts and comes up without his knowing how. The ground of itself produces" (Mark 26:28a).

Early in his ministry Jesus tells Nicodemus that no one can see the kingdom of God unless he is born again from above. It is a spiritual experience, he explains. Like the wind whistling around the corner, we hear the evidence of it but we know not whence it comes or whither it goes. So it is when one is born of the spirit.

Then on a later occasion we find Jesus turning to the parable in order to show this same characteristic of the kingdom. As he so often did, he again draws the illustration from the common life of country folk. Jesus reminds his hearers that the farmer is utterly dependent on nature for his crop. He sows the seed, then goes on about his daily life, unmindful of the marvelous transformation going on under the surface of the ground. Then, lo and behold, the seed has given forth life and a new plant appears. How does it happen and when did it take place? Jesus says simply that the earth produces fruit "of itself." Human effort is limited to planting the seed. One must await the deliberate and leisurely course of the growing process—the blade, the head, the full grain in the ear—before pushing in with a sickle and harvesting the crop which nature has provided.

Jesus emphasizes that the kingdom of God is an inner experience. Here he shows that it is also an experience which only the Heavenly Father can bring about. He alone can perform the miracle of a regenerated heart. In some mysterious way, known only to God, a person is born into the kingdom. Only spread the message, says Jesus, and it will take root in the human heart and grow. God alone can bring about a fruitful result.

How well does Jesus know this to be true! This kingdom of God, this life-giving experience, can only be had as it is imparted by him who is the source of life. That is the way Jesus obtained it; he knows that others must likewise enter the kingdom through an encounter with God. While it is true that Christ himself must bring one to this encounter, it must be a personal experience. Jesus is the way, the door, the Savior, but he is not satisfied until we have the same fellowship with the Father which he has. Do not be astonished, he tells Nicodemus, when I tell you that you must be born again; that is the nature of the kingdom of God. And so, he says, it is like one who only sows the seed, but while sleeping and rising day by day the good earth of itself produces the crop, including the magic alchemy of plant growth and maturing. Who can chart the journey of a Christian into the kingdom of God?

Like Unto a Growing Plant

The kingdom of heaven may be compared to a mustard seed which a man took and sowed in his field. It is the smallest of all seeds, but when it is grown it is the largest of plants; yea, it grows into a tree, so that the wild birds come and roost in its branches (Matt. 13:31b-32).

The kingdom of God *grows*. Jesus continually stresses this aspect of his message. At times it is the central thought, as in the parables of the mustard seed and the leaven. More often the idea of growth is just assumed; it is inherent in the teaching. For example, in the parable of the sower Jesus' whole thought rests upon the fact, taken for granted, that the seed which falls upon good soil *grows*, while that which falls upon stony ground *fails to grow*. Some have no chance to grow because the birds eat them, and still other seed grows but is choked out by weeds. Similar assumptions are contained in the parable of the wheat and the tares: "Let them both grow together until harvest time" (v. 30).

In still another story, the one about the man who sows the seed and awaits the harvest while "the ground of itself produces," Jesus inserts a lovely description which stands out boldly in the pattern. He speaks of the ground putting forth "first the stalk, then the head, at last there is the matured grain of wheat in the head" (Mark 4:26-28). While not the main theme of the parable, this vignette of growing life, with its unfolding stages, must have appealed to Jesus. He elaborates to emphasize the point that, of course, the kingdom must grow.

Whether we consider the kingdom of God in its social

context, as Jesus sometimes does, or as individual experience, which is the emphasis in *A Love That Heals*, we are impressed with its dynamic quality. As for the social concept of the kingdom, history bears witness to the amazing vitality of the program launched by Jesus Christ. The analogy of the mustard seed has been exemplified in the world through these twenty centuries. The leavening influence of the gospel in society never ceases to impress both Christians and unbelievers. The kingdom of God is a ferment—growing, expanding, active, and vital.

Jesus places still more emphasis on the kingdom of God as personal experience. His gospel comes from the deep wells of his own experience. His life with the Father is an ever-increasing enrichment in fellowship as he yields himself constantly to God's will in response to the revelation given to him. He knows the meaning of spiritual growth. He thinks of it in terms of the tender plant, the formative grain, and the full grain in the ear. His message of the kingdom clearly contains this challenge to quality growth. Thus the individual disciple must *progress* in the kingdom experience, for the laws of the realm require it. The vital quality is inherent in the kingdom of God. Like all life, it can live only if it grows. Likewise, without the personal growth of Christ's disciples there will be no kingdom growth in the world. In this important sense the personal and social aspects of the kingdom of God merge into one.

4
Adventuring in Faith

Testimony

So then I tell you, whenever you pray and ask for anything, have faith that it has been granted you, and you will get it (Mark 11:24).

It was in the spring of 1953. I had suffered my second heart attack in the previous December, about a year after the first one. But this time I had not pulled out of it as before. The doctor had prescribed the usual time for hospitalization, and, after that, convalescence at home. I had resumed a light schedule of teaching, but my general vitality did not return. There were days when I was hardly able to finish the lecture while seated at the desk before a small class. Some days, being completely exhausted, I would dismiss the class early.

I was naturally concerned about my failure to recover, and was greatly depressed. In March I received news of the death of my aged father but was unable to make the trip to attend his funeral, and this added further to my depressed feelings. By mid-April I was finding it increasingly difficult to carry on with my one class, but feared that if I gave it up it would be the end of my teaching career.

During these months I did considerable reading on the subject of prayer. I read what others claimed to have discovered about the power of prayer—people of unquestioned integrity who recorded their experiences in modest but con-

65

vincing language. I also reviewed with special interest the great things which were wrought through prayer in Bible times. Above all, there was Jesus, the perfect man of prayer, going about demonstrating its power and saying to me continually through the pages of the Book that this was also for me if I could muster enough faith. I became more intimately acquainted with him as the Lord who is the same yesterday, today, and forever. That being so, then why couldn't I claim the promise? The thought would not leave me: why not?

On the last Sunday morning in April I was alone at home. The week had been rough; I wasn't sure I could make it through the next week of classes. Laying aside the Testament I was reading, I thought: *do I have the faith for this? If I ask, lacking faith, I cannot expect results—except the result of shattered morale. Dare I try it? How is faith generated?* Then, kneeling, I summoned all the faith I possibly could and prayed: Dear Lord, I believe it is your will that I recover enough to get back on my feet again. Please do it for me—*and now I thank you for having done it.*

When my wife returned from church, she asked casually how I felt and I replied, "I feel all right *now,* I'm getting well." She seemed to sense nothing different, probably attributing my remark to my usual forced optimism. But I was determined to believe that it *was* different. I knew at that time that it was going to be different.

Monday's class seemed to be easier for me, but Monday was usually a good day after the weekend rest. Yet, I had a feeling of reserve strength, and it was associated with God's special concern for me. That feeling remained with me through the week, and it was an easy week. By the week's end people were remarking that I "looked better." For the first time in months I was able to put enthusiasm into my teaching. By the second week after that memorable Sunday morning I was "back on my feet again," and continued thereafter to maintain my greatly improved health. True, I continued to live under limitations, and I have also suffered subsequent heart attacks. But I never returned to the state of vitiated health which characterized my condition in the early months of 1953.

I did not ask God for a new circulatory system; I asked for a certain measure of health and it was granted me. I do not claim to understand the change, I only record my own experience. Furthermore, it is but one of several instances in my life which have provided for me a lively adventure in faith. It constitutes another milestone in the spiritual journey which I am endeavoring to trace in these pages.

The Key to the Kingdom

Then Jesus answered them, "Have faith in God!" (Mark 11:22).

Experiences such as the one described in the previous meditation enabled me to enter more fully into the adventures of those who encountered Jesus in Palestine. The episodes in the Gospels in which Christ performs great works through faith had formerly seemed far away and unreal to me. Now they have come alive, and as my journey progresses, the people and happenings become very real. I find myself participating in the experiences of the disciples and listening to the words of Christ as though he were speaking directly to me. His emphasis on the importance of faith bears in upon me as a great imperative. In particular, the evidence of his own measureless faith fills me with wonder and amazement.

So it becomes obvious that faith is the key to the kingdom of God. The key also unlocks the secret of the miracles of Jesus.

Jesus gives much and he asks little for himself, but he says to us all: You must have faith if I am to help you.

In the Gospels, Jesus is always quick to respond to genuine faith. His spirit is sensitive to it. Jesus recognizes faith wherever it is evident regardless of the circumstances in which it appears. Whether he finds it among his own people or in a Roman soldier, whether in a Samaritan woman or a Canaanitish mother, he always rejoices to see the evidence of a trusting heart.

Repeatedly he urges people to have faith, to believe. He chides them for their lack of faith. He reminds them that faith casts out fear. He knows that mountains of apparent obstacles can be removed with faith. He knows the meaning of faith in its purest form—the simple trust of a little child. Finally, he asks people to have faith in him, to believe in him as the Son of God.

One does not journey far into the kingdom of God before becoming aware of this vital quality. If he continues in the Way, he will soon find himself breathing deeply the fresh ozone of faith.

Only Believe

But Jesus paid no attention to what was said, but said to the leader of the synagogue, "Do not be afraid; only keep up your faith" (Mark 5:36).

When Jairus comes to Jesus with a desperate appeal to heal his daughter, Jesus goes with him because of his faith. Jairus appears confident that Jesus can heal his daughter, and his entire attitude manifests a faith which the Master always rejoices to see. On the way they are impeded by the crowd.

Many people press against Jesus, but one touches his garment in faith. He stops abruptly because he must find that person. No one goes unrecognized who comes to Jesus in faith. When the woman who has touched him makes herself known, he says to her: "My daughter, your faith has cured you. Go in peace and be free from your disease" (v. 34).

Meanwhile word comes to Jairus that his daughter has died. Jesus reassures him with the words: "Do not fear, only keep up your faith." Only a moment before he has told the woman that faith releases power; now he is saying that faith will replace fear. Over and over again both facts are demonstrated in the words and deeds of the Master as he goes about his ministry. Jairus must be feeling his own faith being buoyed up by the faith and assurance of Jesus as they go on their way together.

Our faith likewise is sustained when we walk with Jesus. Our reward will be no less today than was that of Jairus in seeing his little daughter restored to life and health. And why not? Jesus Christ is the same today as yesterday. History has not been able to hold him. Was it easier for Jairus to have faith because he knew Jesus in the flesh? We, too, may know him. He becomes real to his followers as we walk with him in daily life. His words, "only keep up your faith," are meant for us in the twentieth century, as well as for a humble ruler of a Jewish synagogue in the time of Rome. If we but believe, we can experience the greater miracle of spiritual resurrection. He will raise us up to life abundant.

No Down Payment

I tell you, I have not found in a single case among the Jews, so great faith as this! (Luke 7:9b).

The Roman captain whose slave Jesus heals displays a quality of faith which astonishes even Jesus and wins his warmest commendation. The centurion first sends some Jewish elders to intercede with Jesus, then he sends others who meet Jesus on the way to the Roman's house. They deliver his message that he is unworthy for Jesus to come under his roof. "But simply speak the word, and let my servant boy be cured," he says through the messengers.

That is the kind of thing which stirs Jesus. His moments of deepest joy are on occasions such as this. Luke says that "he was astonished," and turned to the crowd with the declaration that he had not found so great faith even in Israel. What is it that pleases Jesus so much? Is it not that the man simply accepts him at his word? "Simply speak the word" (v. 7), he has urged Jesus. Here is a manifestation of the childlike trust which Jesus has commended to his disciples. Here is faith without a down payment, trust without prior evidence. Jesus always responds to such faith. His very nature requires that he recognize it, and he never fails to rejoice in it.

The centurion's attitude also contains a large element of humility, strange to see in a Roman. But that was part and parcel of his faith. There can be no faith without a humble heart. Faith, repentance, and the contrite heart are all of one piece.

In contrast, we find here a reason why our own prayers are often ineffective. A proud and stubborn heart prevents the exercise of faith. We may not even be aware that we have such pride. But we are terribly afraid lest we appear naive. We are not ready to say to Jesus: "Simply speak the word." We want some advance guarantee that our petition will be granted—exactly according to specifications—otherwise we might feel foolish about asking. In reality, we are asking for an Aladdin's lamp which has been factory tested and guaranteed to work. Of course, that is not faith at all. As we learn faith from Christ, we try to cultivate the qualities which are manifested in people such as this Roman officer whose faith wins the Master's warm commendation.

Simple Trust

I thank you, Father, Lord of heaven and earth, for concealing these matters from wise and learned men, and for revealing them to little children. Yes, Father, I thank you that your good pleasure made it so (Luke 10:21).

One of the most significant things Jesus says is recorded in this passage of Luke's Gospel. We so-called "intellectuals" are prone to pass over it lightly, for it pierces our intellectual armor, an important ingredient of which is pride. In our quest for a "rational faith" we naturally move out from the childish stage of mere credulity, but we tend also to throw aside the important quality of childlikeness which is simple trust.

After the seventy come back from their mission, delighted that in Jesus' name they have power even over demons, the Master cautions them not to rejoice about the demons but to be glad that their names are enrolled in heaven. At that moment, says Luke, he is filled with joy and says: "I thank you, Father, Lord of heaven and earth, for concealing these matters from wise and learned men, and for revealing them to little children. Yes, Father, I thank you that your good pleasure made it so." On another occasion Jesus talks to his disciples about their becoming as little children if they would qualify for the kingdom of God. Now, having entrusted his cause to the seventy (most of whom were common people) and the experiment having succeeded so wonderfully, Jesus rejoices and takes heart. It is now evident that the gospel will go forward with the common people. Simple trust is more essential than learning.

Jesus does not imply either here or elsewhere that intellectual attainment disqualifies one for the kingdom of Heaven. But he does recognize that simple trust does not come easy to the "intellectual." Learning might become a barrier which the Christian must surmount. Jesus looks upon wealth in the same way. He does not condemn it, but he is painfully aware that money might keep people from God. So too might learning. Both wealth and learning tend to give a person a sense of independence, a certain freedom from physical danger on the one hand and from mental fears on the other. Self-sufficiency and pride grow easily in these attitudes.

Neither the atmosphere of wealth nor of learning is conducive to deep humility. One has a feeling, as he reads this passage in Luke 10, that these concepts are on the mind of Jesus with new intensity in the light of the recent experience by the seventy missionaries. So, in his characteristic way, he lifts his eyes to heaven and gives thanks to the Father for choosing to have it that way.

Faith Wins Again

So Jesus answered her, "You are a woman of great faith! What you
want will be done for you." And at that very moment her daughter was
healed (Matt. 15:28, GNB).

Occasionally Jesus appears unwilling to accede to some
request, usually for healing, but when the petitioner exhibits
genuine faith he responds joyfully and grants the thing desired.

The case of the Canaanitish woman is one of these. Jesus
brings his close disciples to this border country outside Palestine in order to get some rest. Only in this way can he escape
the throngs of people. Obviously, if he should start his healing
ministry here, his fame would soon spread, and he would not
realize the purpose of the retreat. It is important that he remain
as inconspicuous as possible.

Yet here comes a woman crying after him, imploring his
help for her demented daughter. He tries to ignore her but she
persists. He might have thought: *If I am to begin healing again,
I might more properly be back among my own people where
my mission lies.* With such thoughts perhaps in his mind, he
says to the woman: "It isn't right to take the children's food and
throw it to the dogs." Her reply, "Even the dogs eat the
leftovers that fall from their masters' table," is more than Jesus
can resist. It is an affirmation of faith. It is genuine, wrung from
the suffering of a mother for her child. "You are a woman of
great faith," says Jesus, "What you want will be done for you."
And her daughter was cured.

Faith breaks through all barriers. Jesus knows his earthly
mission to be primarily to his own people, but he recognizes
faith wherever it appears. He is sensitive to it and responds to it
as a compass turns to the pole. Can it be said that God
imposes upon himself this limitation of choice, that he *must*

respond to genuine faith? The answer lies in our relationship of faith with him through his Son, Jesus Christ our Lord.

As of a Child

Then He took the little children into His arms, and as he laid His hands upon them one by one, He tenderly blessed them (Mark 10:16).

In one of the most beautiful passages in all the gospels, we see Jesus blessing the little children. He reproves those who try to discourage parents from bringing their children to him. He is indignant about it and says: "Let the children come to me and stop keeping them from it, for to such as these the Kingdom of God belongs. I solemnly say to you, whoever does not accept the kingdom of God as a little child does, will never get into it at all" (Mark 10:14).

What does Jesus have reference to in declaring that we cannot enter the kingdom of God unless we accept it like a child? He speaks of the *simple trust* which is characteristic of little children. A child's trust is the essence of faith, the kind of faith which makes Jesus rejoice and to which he invariably responds regardless of person, place, or circumstance. How difficult it is for an adult to retain this quality of childlike trust along with a growing maturity of mind! Yet true spiritual maturity has a natural, honest, and childlike trust. One of the many paradoxes of Christian experience is that our efforts to meet God's mind with our own avails only as we come in the trustful confidence as a little child.

Let us not forget that Jesus uses this incident of the children to teach a lesson to grownups. He invites us to look back over the road we have been traveling on our spiritual journey and see if we have discarded something essential to our spiritual health. It may mean a radical readjustment for us as we retrace our way in search of it. But what an exhilarating experience when we rediscover that lost vitamin of spiritual growth, a pure and guileless faith.

Courage to Believe

Have faith in God. I solemnly say to you, whoever says to this mountain, "Get up and throw yourself into the sea" and does not doubt at all in his heart, but has faith that what he says will take place, shall have it (Mark 11:23).

Jesus has a profound awareness that he is cooperating with God in ministering to human needs and challenging the power of evil. This consciousness that God is working with him and through him ("The Son can do nothing by Himself," see John 5:19) gives Jesus courage to believe. It helps to explain his amazing faith. His is faith *in God*. God's power is available for him. When he performs a miracle or some great act of faith, he considers it as evidence of God's mercy, not of his own power.

Faith which rests on the premise of God's grace, therefore, can move mountains. Jesus insists that it is so, and that, given sufficient faith, there is no limit to what may be accomplished through prayer. Perhaps the most emphatic statement to this effect are his words in Mark 11:23. He tells us that if we have enough faith we can say to a mountain: "Get up and throw yourself into the sea," and it will take place. Then he adds: "Whenever you pray and ask for anything, have faith that it has been granted you, and you will get it" (Mark 11:24). Note the present perfect tense, "that it has been granted." Jesus makes these statements with the utmost confidence and assurance. He can do so because he has tried it and it works.

Of course, he never prays for the literal removal of a mountain from the earth's surface. That would be mere exhibitionism, which is repugnant to him. But in his enthusiasm to share his great secret he seizes upon the most impressive hyperbole that comes to mind. No, he does not disturb the hills of Judea. But the mountains of evil which he hurls down, the mountains of sin which he lifts from people's lives, mountains of disease and suffering which are removed from human bodies, mountains of guilt and frustration dissolved in the hands of tyrannical consciences—these constitute wonders far surpassing any earth-moving operation of literal import.

Discarding Crutches

You must believe me, that I am in union with the Father and that the Father is in union with me, or else you must do so because of the very things that I am doing (John 14:11).

A change takes place in the tone of the narrative as it moves toward the climax of passion week. We become aware of a tenseness not present in the fresh eagerness of Jesus' early ministry. Exuberance and joy give way to a more serious atmosphere. The shadow of the cross pervades the later chapters of each of the four Gospels. These changes are reflected in the words of Jesus. More and more his teaching takes on a mystical quality demanding a deeper spiritual response from his hearers, deeper than many were capable of giving.

Jesus insists that he did truly come from God the Father, that he and the Father are one, his words being only an echo of

God's own thoughts, his life an extension of God's very being. He asks people to accept him for what he claims to be, on faith if they can. But if that is too much for them, then accept him on the basis of his godly life, his good deeds, and mighty works.

While Jesus is willing for them to base their faith, if necessary, on the things which he does, his first call is to accept him for who he is, namely, the Son of God, simply because he is God's Son. That is to say, Jesus expects people to be drawn to him by their affinity for his spirit. Those whose minds and hearts cannot respond to spiritual things cannot know Jesus, not because he disowns them but because they are unable to comprehend him. Many times in the last days Jesus emphasizes this. We make the choice, not he. The world chooses to ignore him, hence fails to receive him or experience a life united with him. But to the disciples with him in the upper room, he says: You must believe in me. "Whoever has seen me has seen the Father. . . . I am in union with the Father. . . . You must believe . . . " (John 14:9,11).

Jesus demands the same of us. We are told to believe in him. He offers as his credentials his own spirit which we experience when we accept him on faith. Since he is in union with the Heavenly Father, we too will share that experience through our union with him. Our *experience* then makes any further credentials superfluous. But for those who need a crutch for their initial trust, he submits the evidence of his earthly life and deeds. "Believe me for the very works' sake" (KJV). The Gospels do not declare it, but I seem to hear Jesus assuring us that once we come to him, even because of his works, we shall soon throw the crutch away, for we shall find it unnecessary in the strength which is our own, which flows to us through Christ himself. That is the paradox of faith. That is why faith is a surer, more sufficing way to God than rational processes limited by human inadequacy.

The statement, often seen in religious writing, that faith transcends reason, really doesn't make sense to one who has never acted on it or tried it out. Perhaps the assertion should read: Faith plus experience transcends reason. In the final analysis there is no human authority which supersedes experience. Fortunately, we have the Bible with which to validate our spiritual experiences. We know that our experiences are legitimate when they correspond with the teachings of the Bible. The Bible is also an unfailing guide which leads us into deeper and richer experiences.

Acceptance

Others said, "This is the Christ." But still others said, "The Christ does not come from Galilee, does He? Do not the Scriptures say that the Christ is to spring from David and to come from the village of Bethlehem where David lived?" So the people were divided because of Him (John 7:41-43a).

The incident recorded here in John's Gospel is rich in meaning. John quotes Jesus in the familiar words, "If any man is thirsty, let him come to me and drink." Then John feels it necessary to explain that by this water Jesus means the Spirit. He is referring, John says, to the Spirit which believers will receive after Jesus is glorified. Jesus is speaking in spiritual terms. He is implying thereby that his claims for himself should be judged by spiritual standards. And many do. Some say he is a prophet, others even declare that he is the Christ. They are evaluating Jesus on the basis of spiritual criteria. They are judging by what he is and does.

But others are not satisfied with that kind of reasoning. They must have some more authoritative voice than their own experience, which seems to them too short-lived. They need external proof. So they apply the test of legalism and tradition. "What!" they exclaim, "is the Christ to come from Galilee?" Do not the Scriptures say that he is to come from Bethlehem, David's city? For them it matters not what kind of person he is—his message, his spirit, the evidence that God is with him. Instead, they only demand that the circumstances of his birth satisfy a rigid pattern of prophecy and tradition which itself is subject to varied interpretation. Theirs are geography minds. In contrast to them, others are willing to subordinate the claims of literalism to the reality of personal experience in seeing and knowing the Christ. For this latter group the claims of geography and literal prophecy faded away before the reality of Jesus' life and spirit.

We might dismiss the problem by reminding ourselves that Jesus *was* born in Bethlehem and *also* came out of Galilee. Thus he satisfies the claim of prophecy in full. But to give weight to such claims appears contrary to the desire of Jesus himself. He does not bother to remind the people of his birth at Bethlehem. Had he deemed it wise to rest his claims to the messiahship on any circumstances of his birth, the Gospel writers would surely have recorded it. John especially would have mentioned it in these passages which deal with the problem. But Christ insists that people accept him for what he is and what he can do to help them. "If anyone is thirsty, let him come to me and drink" (v. 37).

The same challenge is given to us today. Let us consider with reverence the evidence concerning Jesus' family lineage, Old Testament prophecy about his coming, or the place and circumstances of his birth. Such evidence may indeed be helpful to buttress our faith. But we accept him as he presents himself. He knows that once we do that and taste of the life abundant we will need no other proof. The living water will reward our faith.

5

Toward an Understanding of Christ

We Would See Jesus

And the Word became flesh and dwelt among us, full of grace and truth (John 1:14a, RSV).

A pilgrimage such as this leads one directly to him who proclaims the Kingdom of Heaven. One becomes unmistakably aware that Jesus is the gospel. He is not merely the center around which events move, he encompasses both events and ideas. The more I study about Jesus, the greater is my desire to understand him. These days I am not reading my Testament from a sense of duty. I am driven by eagerness and desire. Using a modern English translation, I read through one of the four Gospels in one "sitting" (actually I read mostly in bed), then others on the following days, only to go back and start them all again. I never weary of the narratives, they amaze me with their freshness and vitality. From the worn pages, by this time full of marginal notes, emerges the figure of Christ, Son of man and divine Son of God.

I am convinced that the fullest appreciation of Christ can be had by traversing the road by which the early disciples arrive at their discovery of who he was. They first follow Jesus as one who opens up for them a wonderful new life, refreshing and invigorating, filled with spiritual power. But as the full impact of his life bears upon them they are led to fall at his feet and worship him as the divine Son of God. They cannot explain him any other way. For them the divinity of Christ is not a creed but an experience.

In somewhat the same way my own appreciation and understanding of Christ is expanding. Like most Christians, I was introduced to Jesus in childhood as our divine Savior, a fact long ago consummated and, buttressed by centuries of human experience, crystallized into doctrine and creed. Hence I always found it easier to adore him as the Son of God than to apprehend him as the Son of man. True, I was quite aware that he came "in the flesh," lived and walked among men, and was "in all points tempted like as we" (Heb. 4:15, KJV). Yet I must admit that the humanity of Jesus in its vital implications largely escaped me. Having known him first as divine, I suppose I unconsciously refused to admit that he could really be part of humankind.

Now, however, I try to see Jesus as a *person*, someone who has something to say to me out of his own personal experience as a human being. I am able to divest myself of the false image of a unique personage who moved through life fully protected against sin and error by a mantle of divinity. To the Bible's testimony that Jesus did not sin I add the all-important reminder that he *could* have sinned. In all reverence I want to know *why* he did not, how he could live a fully victorious life. That is the same question the disciples must have asked themselves and the result is the same for me that it was for them. "But whom say ye that I am?" he asks them, and through Peter as spokesman they answer, "Thou art the Christ" (Matt. 16:15-16, KJV). From their own experience and not by his telling them they acclaimed him the Christ.

So it is that my belief about Christ is verified by a deeper personal knowledge and experience than heretofore. It is less a creed than a conviction. It is not acceptance only, but assurance. I have come to a better knowledge of Christ through (1) association with Jesus the man and (2) an experience of Jesus the Christ.

Like the Greeks who come to Philip saying, "Sir, we want to see Jesus" (John 12:21), I, too, boldly seek a personal interview. What I obtain is a place along side of the Master as he walks among the people, and an opportunity to sit at his feet with his close disciples. The notes which comprise this section represent only a few of my impressions. It is impossible to take the full measure of Christ. But the challenge in such an effort lies in the limitless possibilities of personal growth.

Everyman

But who is my neighbor? (Luke 10:29*b*).

A lawyer comes to ask Jesus about the assurance of eternal life. "What is written in the law?" asks Jesus. "You must love the Lord your God," says the man, "with your whole heart, your whole soul, your whole strength, and your whole mind, and your neighbor as you do yourself." Ah, yes, love! That is the great word: that is God himself, our Heavenly Father. Jesus' response is quick and warm: "You have answered correctly. Continue to do this, and you will live." And I am sure that he intends it to mean: You will live now as well as eternally.

But the questioner is still bothered; the law says to love your neighbor. "But who is my neighbor?" "*Who*," did you say? As though it were a matter of selection, choosing certain people or groups who may be determined in advance—limited, classified in true legal form. Then comes the great masterpiece of the parables, the story of the good Samaritan, which should be called, instead, the story of Everyman. For the central figure, the one who was robbed, beaten, and later befriended, is neither Samaritan, priest, nor Levite, but simply "a man." He was Jesus' answer to the question, "Who is my neighbor?" Unnamed, unidentified, he is still "my neighbor," he is Everyman.

It is a reference to love which prompts this matchless story from the lips of the Master. But love can have no meaning except in terms of human relations. With Jesus, love is not merely a mystical, abstract thing. Love is a dynamic, active force, finding expression in unselfish service. "Who is my neighbor?" the lawyer had asked. "Oh," says Jesus in effect, "it is a matter of *being* a neighbor, not of *finding out who* your neighbor is. Love does not ask who, but only how it can help, comfort, and serve."

Jesus says that God himself is love. He also says that God is spirit. Thus love is the very essence of spiritual reality. The great apostle says the same when he writes that faith, hope, and love "abide"; they endure forever. So, when we are living out love in our everyday relationships, being neighbor to Everyman, we are partaking of eternal life. What we are and do at these times is eternal, it abides.

First Principles

Pay Caesar, therefore, what belongs to Caesar, and pay God what belongs to God (Matt. 22:21b).

They ask Jesus what he thinks about paying taxes to the

Roman Empire: "Is it right to pay the poll tax?" *Here is a good chance to embroil him in politics,* they think. He can easily get himself involved with the government, or, if he plays it safe with Rome, he can be made to appear as a collaborationist. In either case he stands to lose. His reply surprises and amazes them, "And they left Him and went away."

But more than anything else his reply reveals again the quality of his thinking and his scale of values. This incident is sometimes used to suggest that Jesus approved Roman rule, or at least that he disapproved any violation of established authority. In reality it does not say anything about his views on government except that he refuses to take a position either for or against Rome. He says to pay the tax to Rome, but that does not commit him on the basic question of loyalty. Jesus is indifferent to political questions of the day. His mission and message transcend politics. In this particular incident he skillfully parries a tricky question and refuses to become involved in politics. He declares that the taxation that really matters is our response to the claims of the kingdom of God.

His mission is immeasurably more important than the problem of Roman rule over Judea. Empires rise and fall with monotonous sequence in history. Rome has long since disappeared, but the spiritual kingdom which Jesus established still endures. When he says "Pay Caesar, therefore, what belongs to Caesar, and pay God what belongs to God," his mind is centered more on the latter than the former. His interests are spiritual. He is a citizen of a government without taxation. He will pay the tax, yes, because it belongs to Caesar—Rome's fee for governing. But that is quite incidental with Jesus; everything really belongs to God, life itself belongs to God.

Paying God what belongs to him is the preeminent concern, our all-encompassing purpose. With Jesus it is a consuming passion. The political sway of the Roman Empire, bound within the strict limits of time, is a trifling matter in comparison with the abiding values of the kingdom of God.

Tuning In

Let him who has ears to hear with, listen! (Luke 8:8b).

Jesus frequently says in the course of his teaching, "He that hath ears to hear, let him hear" (KJV). Williams's translation reads that "he exclaimed, 'Let him who has ears to hear with, listen!' " Later he tells his disciples that, while they are permitted to know the secrets of the kingdom of God, others must receive them in figurative language, "so that they may look and not see, may hear and not understand."

This certainly is not of Christ's choosing. His love encompasses every person in the throng which follows him. He would have everyone enter into the kingdom of God and enjoy the priceless privilege of citizenship therein. The passion of his life is to help people to know the Father as he knows him. But such knowledge and such experience cannot be given to others as one might give a gift. They are matters of the inner life. Jesus cannot transmit to anyone intact the spiritual perception needed to comprehend and experience the kingdom of God. One's heart must be attuned to the message else one will hear it without understanding it.

We know that spiritual perception seems to be more alive in some people than it is in others. But it is also true that Christians experience times when they are more attuned to God's voice than usual. In these periods of study, worship, prayer, or service we grasp what earlier we heard but failed to understand. The secrets of the kingdom of God do not require a special code for their understanding, but rather a trusting and obedient heart.

To assume, therefore, that religious experience is for some and not for others is foreign to the spirit of Christ. Spiritual aptitude is not to be considered as a permanent trait like an intelligence quotient. While Jesus laments that so many looked without really seeing, he constantly seeks to open their spiritual eyes that they might *all* see. If the door to the kingdom is closed to us, it is because of our own choosing. We ourselves are at the controls in this case. We can turn the dial of our minds and hearts and tune in to the frequency wave of Christ's spirit.

Living Water

The woman said to Him, "I know that the Messiah is coming, the One who is called the Christ. When He comes, He will tell us everything!" Jesus said to her, "I, the very one who is talking to you, am He!" (John 4:25-26).

In the encounter with the Samaritan woman, Jesus reveals his true self. We see the driving force in his life, his dominant desires. For in this brief meeting with a low caste woman Jesus spontaneously shares his deepest insight with one who does not feel herself to be worthy of his notice. It is his very meat and drink to do that. "I have food to eat of which ye do not know," he tells his disciples, and adds in explanation, "My food is to do the will of Him who sent me."

It is entirely natural for him to speak this way. For Jesus the spiritual values are everything; temporal matters count little. It is natural for him to speak about the "living water" (spiritual life) as transcending the water from Jacob's well. He knows that the temporal things of life fade into the background of importance when one drinks of this living spirit, which, like a fresh spring, is continually bubbling up to permeate one's life with joy and peace and righteousness, that is, with eternal life. Moreover, he claims that he can give that living water. The words, "that I will give," are spoken in the confidence that he is able to carry out his promise. One of the marvelous things about Jesus is his absolute certainty that, with his help, others can experience the same exhilarating happiness which he knows. He never once doubts his mission.

Jesus interprets his mission in terms of giving a spiritual meaning to life. He is particularly conscious of it on the day that he meets the Samaritan woman at Jacob's well. When she seeks to evade his reference to her personal life by raising an old ecclesiastical controversy—whether to worship on the Samaritan mountain or in the Jewish Temple—Jesus deftly lifts the theme again to the high plane of true spiritual worship. "God is a spiritual Being," he tells her, "and His worshipers must worship Him in spirit and reality." Spiritual communion with the Father, not place-bound ceremonialism, defines our worship. Otherwise, worship has no meaning for Jesus and should have none for us.

In this connection Jesus is meeting his old enemy, the legalistic mind, which has encased the religious life of the Jews and has all but smothered the vital spark of faith. Here in rural Samaria, far from the elaborate Temple ritual of Jerusalem, the pervading evil confronts him. His words seem to rise with vehemence: "God is a spirit" (KJV). Like the old prophets before him, Christ seeks to lift his people out of the deadening meshes of formalism in order that they might stand free and strong on the solid ground of personal experience and an inner religion.

Such considerations form the background for the great declaration which Jesus makes to the woman. She speaks of the Messiah who is coming. "I am he," says Jesus. He later makes this claim to his disciples in connection with his imminent suffering. He admits it to Pilate and the Jewish leaders on the day of his crucifixion. Here, too, he reveals himself as Christ, and he does so in the context of reiterating that religion is a personal experience, and not merely formal worship.

The meaning of his words to the woman at the well is exemplified in the experience of the townspeople. After hearing Jesus, they told her: "It is no longer because of your statement that we believe, for we have heard him ourselves, and *we know*. . . . " Only as we experience Christ can we know him, and, knowing him, we can worship God as we should.

"But whoever drinks the water that I will give him will never, no never be thirsty again" (John 4:14*a*).

Pure Gold

So Jesus said to him, as He saw that he had answered thoughtfully, "You are not far from the kingdom of God!" (Mark 12:34).

How often beauty rises out of rough and rugged surroundings. So, too, does love often find its greatest expression in the midst of hate and evil. Mark 12:28-34 is one of the most beautiful gems of the New Testament, not only because of its majestic theme but also in that its beauty is enhanced by the setting in which it is placed.

Jesus on this occasion is being hard pressed by his enemies. The Sadducees and Pharisees gang up against him. They come at him with tricky questions designed to trap him into making some statement which can be twisted and used as a charge against him. Their purpose is evil and the atmosphere is charged with hatred. Surely Jesus' soul is harried by their sniping attacks. He is doubtless weary in the presence of such behavior.

Then out of this welter of malice and hate comes a question which he recognizes at once as sincere, which he need not parry, and which he can meet with directness and enthusiasm. A scribe wants to know what, in Jesus' opinion, is the greatest Commandment. Being a good legalist by training, he is naturally interested in getting everything in its proper classification. And so he asks: "Master, which commandment is the greatest?" Jesus is *not* a legalist, and he is not interested in getting *everything* in its proper classification. But he does know that God's truth is based on a deep, fundamental unity and that at the very heart of the universe is a God of love. Therefore, he hastens to meet the question. We can almost see the situation changing from a verbal skirmish to mutual understanding as Jesus eagerly responds.

Love is first above everything. Love is the essence of God himself. So, reaching deep into Scripture, Jesus holds up to view a gem of pure gold: The first commandment is to love your God. Love him with all your heart, soul, mind, and strength. That is the greatest of all the Commandments. Then, reaching again into the same treasure chest, he lifts out a second gem to go along with the first: you must love your neighbor as yourself. "No other command," says Jesus, "is greater than these." Years later the great apostle, writing to the church at Corinth, echoes Jesus' words with his great summation: "And the greatest of these is love."

The dialogue of Jesus and the scribe continues to a significant conclusion. The latter, agreeing heartily with what Jesus has said, adds his own comment that to love one's God and one's neighbor "is far more than all the burnt-offerings and sacrifices." Is he still trying to get everything classified and in its proper place? At any rate, whether he realizes it or not, he has struck at the roots of the controversy over this Jesus of Nazareth. He is actually preaching the "good news." He is placing inner life and attitudes above outward forms. He is saying that it is more important to be than to do. Jesus had been saying those things for years, they are the very heart of his gospel. No wonder, then, that he replies to the scribe: "You are not far from the kingdom of God."

Compassion

As they were leaving Jericho, a great crowd followed Him. And two blind men sitting by the roadside heard that Jesus was passing and cried out, "Do pity us, Lord, you Son of David!"

And Jesus stopped and called them, and asked, "What do you want me to do for you?"

They answered Him, "Lord, we want our eyes opened!" Then Jesus' heart was moved with pity, and He touched their blinded eyes, and at once they could see again, and followed Him (Matt. 20:29-34).

In these half-dozen verses is a picture of beauty and compassion. It is as if we turned the page of the Bible and found there a lovely sketch designed to illustrate the text. It shows Jesus walking along the Jericho road, followed by a large crowd of people. Seated by the roadside are two men whose names are still unknown. They do not count as real men anyway, for they are just a burden to society. Their lives are blunted; they live in darkness. They belong to that sorrowful company of the blind.

Hearing that it was Jesus who was passing, they call out to him. They do not see him, they can only hear. Lack of sight does not dull their inner vision nor the hope that seizes them. They are filled with excitement mingled with fear lest this opportunity slip away from them. This is their great moment; on it hangs their hope of freedom from a prison of darkness. They simply must gain his attention. "Son of David," they shout, "Do pity us, Lord." "Hush," they are told in effect, "Pipe down, you fellows, this is the great Rabbi." But theirs is a cry of distress, a call of utter desperation. Moreover, it has in it the vital note of faith. I think that is why Jesus hears them; his ears are always turned to the frequency wave of believing hearts. He stops. Then he calls to them and asks them a question: "What do you want me to do for you?"

I wonder why Jesus asks those sightless men such a question as that. Their need is obvious; Jesus needs no help from them to understand the deep desire of their hearts. Yet he puts the question to them. It must be that he needs their response, their cooperation. It is always a two-way transaction when Jesus helps anyone. Actually, the question is not superfluous but necessary. It elicits from the men their eager petition: "Lord, we want our eyes opened."

"Your Father knows what you need before you ask Him" (Matt. 6:8), Jesus has taught us. Yet we must ask. Moreover, we must learn to ask in faith. The Father does indeed know what we need and is eager to supply it. But is it not strange that he is unable to do it until we come to him with trustful heart and humble spirit? God cannot satisfy our spiritual hunger unless we ask him. But, as James reminds us, "Draw near to God and He will draw near to you" (4:8).

So it is as Jesus passes along the road leading out of Jericho, he takes time out to answer a call for help. There he stands in the foreground of the scene, with a look of compassion, touching their eyes so that they receive their sight.

His Joy

And He turned to His disciples when they were alone, and said,
"Blessed are the eyes that see what you are seeing. For I tell you, many
prophets and kings have wished to see what you are seeing, but they
could not, and to hear what you are hearing, but they did not" (Luke
10:23-24).

The spontaneous joy of the Master is evident throughout the
record of his life. It comes from the deep inner springs of his
soul. His is a happy life because of that quality emanating from
the kingdom of God within. Joy is a vital ingredient of the
kingdom life.

This invigorating and contagious good cheer is especially
evident in Jesus' life during the earlier periods of his ministry.
But there comes a time when God reveals to him the full
meaning of the messiahship in terms of suffering and martyr-
dom. Do we find less of joy and happy exuberance in Jesus
after that? We sense, indeed, grief and sorrow, but the joy is
still there, only deeper and more intense.

After the events surrounding the transfiguration there is
evident in the gospel narrative a dominant note of seriousness
as God's plan becomes clear to Jesus and the cross looms up
before him. The change is obvious as he seeks to prepare the
twelve also for the crisis which lies ahead. We note especially a
sense of urgency in sending out the seventy. The program
must be launched at once for the time is growing short. A large
group is assembled—people who are no doubt carefully
selected but who have not shared the intimate association with
the Master which the twelve have known. It is clearly an
experiment. The spreading of the kingdom message is to be
entrusted to the laity. After detailed instructions they are sent
out in twos. Their message is to be repentance and the
kingdom of God. Can they measure up to it? Will the plan
succeed?

It is in connection with this effort to launch the program of world evangelism, and against the background of crisis and foreboding, that we find the most unrestrained expression of pure joy on the part of Jesus. The seventy come back full of enthusiasm, reporting great success. The experiment has received the approval of God. Luke 10:21 states that Jesus "rejoiced in the Holy Spirit" (RSV). This special delight is firmly linked with that which is nearest his heart, namely, the kingdom of God. He shares the enthusiasm of the missionaries who are delighted in the evidence of God's power. They themselves experienced the kingdom of God more deeply as they carried it to others. With joy and thankfulness Jesus turns instinctively to his Heavenly Father and pours out his thanks.

This experience is not just a passing mood for Jesus, as is seen by the fact that his happiness continues to glow in his heart after the incident has passed. Later, when he is alone with his disciples, we find him still talking about it. "Blessed are the eyes that see what you are seeing," he tells them. You are more fortunate, he says, than the godly men of old who longed to see and hear evidence that the kingdom of God can truly reign in human hearts. Because the disciples are seeing it, they too are filled with joy.

Credentials

Go and tell John what you hear and see: the blind are seeing and the crippled are walking, the lepers are being healed and the deaf are hearing, the dead are being raised and the poor are having the good news preached to them (Matt. 11:4-5).

Jesus makes it clear that he knew himself to be truly the Messiah, God's son, the world's Savior. One way he reveals his messiahship is through his works. When John the Baptist sends some of his own disciples to ask Jesus to tell them if he is really "the one who was to come," what reply does Jesus send the rugged man of God confined behind Herod's prison walls? He gives John a demonstration of what the Messiah should be and do. He replies not by authority but by evidence, not fiat but confirmation. And what does the evidence consist of? Healing the blind, the lame, the lepers, the deaf, raising the dead to life, and preaching the good news to the poor.

These are the credentials for messiahship which Jesus submits to John. He might have spoken of his genealogical lineage or the miraculous circumstances of his birth. He could have reminded John of the assuring voice at the time of his baptism, for John had shared that experience with him. He might have sent John a full brochure of testimony concerning God's favor toward him, including evidence that he was truly baptizing with the Holy Spirit as John had foretold. But Jesus chooses to use other proofs. He rests his case on the grounds of humanity. He has come to seek and to save people. People are being healed and the poor are being given the gospel.

This, then, is what Jesus says in effect to John: "See, I am giving them life—physical healing and the secret of abundant life in fellowship with the Father. I rest my claim on who I am, on the facts of experience, on my own life and ministry." Only then, after presenting himself to John's disciples through his ministry of love and service, does Jesus finally give an affirmative answer to John's question: "How happy are those who have no doubts about me!" (v. 6, GNB). In other words, "Blessed are you, John, if you can accept me on the basis of the evidence which I am giving you."

We have no record of John's response. But in the tribute which Jesus immediately pays to John at the time I think we can see not only a eulogy directed to the audience before

Jesus, but also a challenge for John's disciples to take back to their master. John is greater than all the prophets, he is on the very threshold of the kingdom of God. Can he step across the line and actually bridge the remaining distance between the old dispensation and the new? I believe that Jesus beckons him to take that very step.

A Love That Heals

So Jesus asked him, "What is your name?" And he answered, "Legion!" For many demons had gone into him (Luke 8:30).

When Jesus approaches the raving maniac in the country of the Gerasenes, he says or does something which causes an immediate reaction in the man. Luke says he commands the foul spirits to get out of the man. I wonder if it is not Jesus' manner rather than the words he speaks which brings the tormented man to a sudden realization that he faces a physician of the spirit. Is Jesus' manner harsh and peremptory? We might be led to think so, since he has to "command" the foul spirits. But I believe that it is actually just the opposite. *Jesus heals the man by means of love.* He approaches him with such love and compassion that the tempestuous spirit of the madman is subdued in the presence of the stronger force. When Jesus says to the man, "What is your name?" I believe he speaks in a quiet voice and in a manner that is calm and reassuring. Love and compassion go out from Jesus and so encompass the troubled spirit of the man that he begins to feel a strong peace. Jesus loves him just as he has loved that other young man, the "rich young ruler," who is so much more lovable. The difference between our human love and the unbounded love of God is just this: God loves also the unlovable.

Looking a little further into the method of the Master, why does he ask the man the question, "What is your name?" Is it to elicit the reply about the legion of foul spirits so that Jesus can then deal with them? Or is it for a deeper reason? If one has a name he has identity, he *is* somebody, he can begin to relate himself to others. To recall his own name will help him become aware of himself, his own personality. The very essence of Christ is his feeling of concern for every individual, his respect for the intrinsic value of each human soul. When he suggests to this man that he does have a name, an identity, in spite of the legion of demons which hold him prisoner, the Master is, by that very means, helping the man break out of his prison into the free air of sanity.

Glorify Your Father in Heaven

Let your light shine before people in such a way that they may see your good deeds, and praise your Father in heaven (Matt. 5:16).

Jesus is moved by one great passion above all others, namely, to glorify God the Father. It is apparent throughout the Gospels. The idea of glorifying your Father in heaven is frequent in his teachings. The prayer which he teaches his disciples, which we know as the Lord's Prayer, begins and ends with praise to God. His sincere desire, the great motivation of his life, is to give thanks and praise to his Heavenly Father.

Jesus believes this to be the supreme goal for humankind. Even one's salvation from sin cannot be separated from this goal, for when we ask to what end we are saved, we must look for an ultimate purpose, and we find it in bringing honor to the Father in heaven. Jesus makes it clear that our destiny is to be fulfilled in the glory and honor which we bring to the Creator. He assumes that his hearers accept his premise; his own avowal of it is almost casual.

The Gospel writers often mention that the popular response to Jesus' acts of mercy is to praise God, to give thanks to God, or to glorify the Father. "Glorify your Father which is in heaven" is part of the Hebrew heritage which is woven into the fabric of the gospel. Like many other priceless jewels, it comes from the treasure house of Old Testament truth. But Jesus lifts it out and gives it added luster in the setting of his own higher revelation.

Living in the kingdom of God we are alive to this as one of the great imperatives. We subordinate all other goals in life to second place. Our most worthy objectives, our noblest purposes are evaluated by what we accomplish. To grasp the full import of that goal—to glorify God the Father—to feel it in one's being as a genuine urge, is truly a high experience. It is to be greatly desired and sought after. Jesus looks at his own ministry in this way. If we can catch this portion of Christ's spirit and weave it into the pattern of our thought and action, we will have come close to the secret of his life and his gospel.

Spiritual Portrait

So this is the way you must pray:
Our Father in heaven,
Your name be revered,
Your kingdom come,
Your will be done on earth as it is done in heaven.
Give us today our daily bread for the day,
And forgive us our debts, as we have forgiven our debtors;
And do not let us be subjected to temptation,
But save us from the evil one (Matt. 6:9-13).

Although the Lord's Prayer is one of the richest gems in the Bible, its radiance is dulled for most of us by formal repetition. We learned it in childhood, and have generally treated it as a prayer to be "said" in unison. Doubtless we have been guilty of the very thing Jesus warns against. When he gives this prayer to the disciples, he cautions them not to use vain repetitions as do the heathen, who think they will be heard for their much speaking.

A fresh approach to these familiar verses is to view the passage in the context of the entire discourse of which it is a part, and in relation to all that Jesus teaches. We see it then as the natural expression of his thought and spirit. We see that the ideas contained in this prayer do not appear there for the first time, or the last; they pervade the whole chapter and the entire Gospel as well. The petitions are altogether spontaneous as Jesus speaks them, reflecting his inmost desires.

Thus a segment of Scripture which heretofore has been something of a ritual, or has come to us as a gem of music, however lovely, now appears as a revelation of the deep inner life of the Lord Jesus—a spiritual portrait as it were. It is a self-portrait, a word picture revealing the Master's true likeness. Although given as a Model Prayer for the disciples, it is in a true sense the *Lord's* prayer, for the petitions are the very essence of his soul's sincere desire.

What are the features of this portrait? How does it reveal the characteristics of the subject? There is first of all the spirit of adoration and praise to the Heavenly Father. How characteristic of Jesus, whose supreme desire is to glorify the Father! It is a desire which is manifest throughout the Gospel narratives. Truly the words "Hallowed be thy name" (KJV) come naturally to Jesus.

How better can one glorify God than to seek earnestly to do his will? From early life Jesus seeks it, and he can say that his will is one with the Father's. At Gethsemane he is able to say "Your will be done" because he has been saying it all his life. In the Lord's Prayer the words are more revealing of his spirit than the most skillful touch of an artist's brush on canvas.

If Jesus has a passion to do his Father's will, he is equally concerned to see it done by people everywhere. This means the establishment of the kingdom of heaven, the rule of the spirit in mind and heart. He talks more about this than any other subject. His program is to usher in the kingdom. When he prays, "Your Kingdom come," another feature is added to the portrait.

It is a spiritual portrait. Accordingly, the needs of the body are discernible only in the background. "Give us today our daily bread for the day." That is all. Wealth has no place in his life; his joy does not depend on things. His Heavenly Father knows his needs and he walks in faith. In that trust he asks only for daily bread.

The reference to physical need gives way to a more vital concern, the concern for right relationships with others. "Forgive us . . . as we have forgiven." An unforgiving heart, so destructive of character—and character is the most important goal in life—is Jesus' great concern. He says more about it in the verses immediately following the prayer. It appears that he selects this feature of the portrait for special comment and interpretation.

Finally, aware of our human frailties, he entreats the Father to lead us not into temptation. Thus far our study reveals a Christ who seems to beckon us upward to high spiritual ground. Now there emerges an understanding Savior, tempted in all points as we, ready to intercede for us and help us overcome. With this feature added, a new dimension appears in the portrait.

The passage closes on another note of praise. Thus the Lord's Prayer begins and ends with expressions of holy reverence. The Holy Spirit who inspires Matthew's writing completes a frame for the portrait. Reaching back to the opening theme, he draws it around the perimeter and encloses the Savior's likeness in a vow of adoration: "For thine is the kingdom, and the power, and the glory, forever. Amen" (v. 13b, KJV).

6

Some Deeper Meanings

Your Kingdom Come

It was just after that that Jesus Christ for the first time clearly taught His disciples that He had to go to Jerusalem and submit to many forms of suffering at the hands of the elders, high priests, and scribes, and be killed, but be raised to life on the third day (Matt. 16:21).

Jesus prays, and teaches his disciples to pray, "Your kingdom come." He must have prayed often for this, for it is the very heart of his message. It is his great concern. He is sure that it is the Father's will.

The Son of God comes to see, however, that a terrible price will have to be paid if the kingdom of God is to become possible on earth. People can never attain it in their own moral or spiritual strength. Only with God's help can one enter into the kingdom and experience salvation. And that must be accomplished through the death of his son, followed by victory over the grave in a mighty demonstration of God's power. All this weighs heavily on the mind of Jesus as, having become aware of the Father's will concerning it, he turns his steps toward the Holy City and the consummation of the divine plan.

Every time I read one of the Gospels through to the end I become freshly aware of two large areas in the earthly ministry of Christ. In the early part, his emphasis is on the kingdom of God, a way of life which brings blessedness and irrepressible joy arising from faith in God and complete confidence in his goodness and care. Later in his ministry, as the forces of hate begin to close in on him, Jesus emerges as the Christ who must suffer and endure the most complete humiliation. On the anvil of suffering the exuberant happiness of his early ministry is transmuted into the joy of which he speaks at the Last Supper. The deep enthusiasm which issues from the Sermon on the Mount is gradually transcended by an even deeper earnestness, the abundant life being absorbed into the mystery of divine suffering. The thrill of new discovery which Jesus himself must feel when he is setting forth the formula for happiness during those busy weeks in Galilee is finally swallowed up in a still more encompassing satisfaction—the peace of fulfillment.

A mystery indeed, the cross of Christ transcends human values and human understanding. The gladness of resurrection morning is a joy born of suffering on the cross. Without the sadness of separation in the upper room, Christ could not have spoken the words which he spoke there: "That the joy which I have had may remain in you and that your joy may be complete" (John 15:11).

And so the full measure of Christ the Savior is revealed as we walk with him on the way to the cross. Our journey will finally carry us to an open tomb on a glorious Easter morning. Then we will be able to leave the narrow confines of history and move on into the spiritual reality of the kingdom of God.

Paradox

If anyone wants to come with me, he must forget himself, carry his
cross, and follow me. For whoever wants to save his own life will lose it;
but whoever loses his life for my sake will find it (Matt 16:24-25, GNB).

Jesus is accepted by his close disciples as the Christ, the one
who is to come. In the question-and-answer session near
Caesarea Philippi, he elicits from them, through Peter as
spokesman, their great affirmation. They recognize the
Messiah by what they see in him, by his life and spirit, not by
his telling them to believe. But after they make their confession
he has much to tell them. He knows it will be hard for them to
accept, as this first lesson demonstrates. He points out that the
messiahship means suffering and death, out of which will come
ultimate victory. He explains to them that the Christ will suffer
all these things.

It is interesting that Matthew uses the title "Jesus Christ" for
the first time in this passage following Peter's confession, and it
is used in connection with Jesus' suffering on the cross. Can it
be said that only in this respect may we think of Jesus as the
Christ? That there could be no Savior except as one who
suffers? He has come into the world on a song of joy sung by
the angels of heaven. He begins his ministry preaching a joyful
message, the promise of life rich and full, which he speaks of as
the kingdom of heaven. But such a salvation can be made
secure for people only through pain and death. Suffering is to
be the price of victory. Mere human effort cannot bring about
such a consummation. The fact that Jesus does accomplish it is
eloquent testimony to the messiahship.

Jesus emphasizes the cross as the saving element in life. As
he is about to be destroyed on the cross he describes it as a
way of life rather than death. As he is about to meet apparent

defeat he describes the cross as a way of victory. He is to be crucified. His followers likewise must deny themselves and each must take up a cross and follow him. If one is to save his life he must lose it. Jesus is asking his disciples to grasp a profound spiritual truth. So just as he lives out his other teachings, he lives this one—laying down his life and taking it up again. The last events of his earthly life constitute a parable of his teachings. His whole ministry receives new meaning by the paradoxical climax whereby victory emerges from seeming defeat.

Creative Suffering

And while they were going down the mountain, He cautioned them not to tell anyone what they had seen until the Son of Man should rise from the dead. And they held their caution fast in their minds as they continued to discuss among themselves what rising from the dead meant (Mark 9:9-10).

After the transfiguration Jesus continues to teach the disciples what the messiahship will mean for him—suffering, rejection, death on a cross, but ultimate victory over the grave.

In this context the transfiguration becomes part of Christ's preparation for the ordeal which lies ahead. (Luke states that Elijah and Moses spoke with him of his imminent death.) It is also for the sake of the three disciples who are with him. Once more they are reassured that this Master is truly God's Son, his beloved. They are unable to understand the experience at that time; its meaning will have to be revealed to them through further experience. Jesus knows that, and on the way down from the mountain he cautions them to tell no one about it until after the Son of man has risen from the dead. Thus the

Master utilizes a principle of pedagogy which is too much neglected by teachers of youth. Truths which the pupil may not fully grasp at once may yet be planted, to be remembered later and understood with the deepening insight of maturity.

Such is the experience of Peter, James, and John. First, Christ will die on the cross and rise again the third day, as he has told them. Then the Holy Spirit will open their minds to the fuller meaning of Christ's suffering. Indeed, the early disciples, like ourselves, continue to learn of Christ and from Christ throughout the remainder of their lives. It is not surprising, then, that of the three who are with Jesus on the mount, two— Peter and John—are to leave significant writings on the meaning of suffering and of growth into spiritual maturity, while James drinks the cup of suffering to become one of the early martyrs. Consider, for example, how Peter, years afterward, is able to write to the Christians of Asia Minor that they should rejoice over their trials as a test of faith, while from the Isle of Patmos the beloved disciple sends his message of comfort and hope to the persecuted churches. From the lessons begun on the mount of transfiguration they advance in the understanding of Christ until they can fling the challenge of faith and hope in the face of any adversity. They are learning how to overcome the world.

Alternative

Now my soul is troubled; what shall I say? Father, save me from this hour of agony! And yet it was for this very purpose that I came to this hour of agony. Father, glorify your name (John 12:27).

When the Greeks come asking for an interview with Jesus, it affects him deeply. They must have opened up before Jesus a vision of a whole new ministry, the mission to the Greek world. What a challenge to the Son of man, whose spirit would respond so eagerly to the freedom-loving Greeks, unencumbered by the shackles of legalistic theology! And he is yet a young man on the very threshold of life. Here is a vista of fruitful service stretching down the years. Most important of all, it offers an escape from the impasse with the Jewish authorities; yes, it must be faced, here is an alternative to the cross.

All this might have flashed through the mind of Jesus as Andrew and Philip bring him the message of the delegation from beyond Palestine. Our Lord is perhaps confronted with the temptation to evade, or at least delay, the awful trial awaiting him.

Immediately, as on previous occasions, the tempter is recognized and thrust back. The Father has revealed to his Son the divine plan. It is laid on different lines—hard lines— leading to seeming disaster. It is a plan based on paradox. It rests on a principle which the world cannot readily comprehend. It involves the apparent defeat of the cause and points straight to the leader's ignominious death. Yet that is the plan; he must not deviate from it. He must resist temptation, even the "temptation" to become a foreign missionary.

Jesus might have been thinking of all that as he replies to Andrew and Philip, "The time has come for the Son of man to be glorified." He is saying that it is not yet time to start the evangelization of the world. That world can be reached only through the crucified and risen Christ. The Greeks must wait for Paul and Barnabas and Silas and Luke and Timothy and a host of believers who were to be made new creatures in Christ through the power of his spirit. But first the Christ must suffer; he must be glorified.

Jesus then proceeds to explain to the people around him

why all this is as it is. "Unless a grain of wheat falls into the ground and dies. . . . Whoever loves his lower life will lose the higher" (vv. 24-25). Such is the pattern of God's truth; it is the law of sacrificial love. It is the key to the master plan of God's purpose in sending his Son. Jesus had long since discovered the key and had accepted the plan.

As he approaches the grim reality, the Son of God who is also the Son of man shrinks from it in human weakness. He, himself, is that seed which must die, he, only thirty-three years old! As this fear grips him he feels the need of reassurance from his Heavenly Father. Breaking forth in prayer he speaks to God rather than to the people in his presence: "Now my soul is troubled: what shall I say? Father, save me from this hour of agony! And yet it was for this very purpose that I came to this hour of agony. Father glorify your name." Then reassurance comes once more in a voice which some think is thunder and others say is an angel speaking to him. Jesus reminds them that it is for their sakes that the voice comes, for "this world is now in process of judgment." That is to say, the master plan is already under way, the plan for the world's redemption. At its center stands the cross, and by the love which will be focused there the Christ will draw all men to himself. "All men" would include the Greeks who are waiting for an answer from Andrew and Philip.

New Wine

He also took the cup of wine and gave thanks; then He gave it to them, saying, All of you drink some of it, for this is my blood which ratifies the covenant, the blood which is to be poured out for many for the forgiveness of their sins (Matt. 26:27-28).

The farewell meeting which Jesus holds with his disciples is to serve a number of purposes. It is the Passover observance, a sacred ritual. It is to be a time of fellowship which Jesus longs to have with those he loves. He will also institute a new rite to be observed by his followers in his memory. At this final session he will have to deal with his betrayer and send him away from the group. The others will need to be fortified against the coming blow and made ready for the crisis. Finally, Jesus will utilize these crucial hours to drive home once again some of the great lessons which the disciples must retain if the kingdom of God is to take root. In particular, the lessons of humility and love must be rooted firmly in their hearts.

The occasion for the meeting arises from the old order, the Jewish Passover feast, but from the first it is obvious that Jesus has his vision fixed on the new day ahead. "I tell you," he says as he initiates the new observance, "I will never again drink the product of the vine till the day when I drink the new wine with you in my Father's kingdom!" (Matt. 26:29). Mark says: " . . . when I drink the new wine in the kingdom of God" (14:25). Luke's record reads: "I shall never again eat one [Passover Supper] until it finds its full fruition in the kingdom of God" (22:16).

It is the kingdom of God that is uppermost in the mind of Christ. His main concern is still the spiritual kingdom which he came to establish on earth, which has been the central theme of his message, which is the subject of most of his parables, and has been in the center of his thought and his prayers through the years of his ministry. It is the new wine of spiritual reality as he has known it in his own life and is determined to share it with humankind. Attitudes, spiritual power in one's life, union with the Father, joy, peace, and happiness—these are all parts of the "new wine" of the kingdom of God to which Jesus has reference. That is the continual feast he shares with us, the fellowship of the spirit.

Quintessence

Love one another. Just as I have loved you, you too must love one another. By this everybody will know that you are my disciples, if you keep on showing love for one another (John 13:34-35).

In his last meeting with the twelve in the upper room, Jesus sums up his central teachings. He wants to impress upon them the very heart of his message. For that reason the passages of John's Gospel which give us this record contain the quintessence of Christianity. The master key is love, all-inclusive love, that which the great apostle later discovers and perfectly defines in the thirteenth chapter of First Corinthians. Love is to be the password for the new order. Love will assure their loyalty to Jesus, and love will hold them together in a unity of spiritual brotherhood. "You must love one another," he tells them, "just as I have loved you."

In connection with this injunction to love he promises to give a helper. Jesus is aware that he is making demands on his followers the like of which no one has ever made before. You *must* love, he insists. But alas, weak and sin-burdened humanity can never measure up unaided to such an ideal. The Holy Spirit must come, therefore. This strange mystery of God's power must be unfolded if people are to love in spite of their humanity. The Advocate, the Helper, the Spirit of Truth—makes it possible for us to follow Christ. We are enabled therewith to enter fully into the kingdom of God.

In everything that Jesus asks of his disciples, he can point to himself as a model for them to follow. "Just as I have loved," he says. Here lies the most extraordinary thing about this extraordinary person, Jesus. He is able to claim perfection of character without the least feeling of boastfulness or self-righteousness. His sensitive conscience, so quick to detect shame and hypocrisy, would never have allowed him to assume a claim to righteousness which he does not possess. Yet he does claim it and can say to his disciples: look to me as your model, and you will come to know God. Why can he say it with such complete self-confidence? The answer is that he knows himself to be one with God—to be God's very chosen, his Son, unique among all humankind. He asserts this as a self-evident fact which the disciples have already accepted.

Jesus feels he has the right to assume that they have accepted it. When Philip reveals that he has fallen short of this spiritual goal, the Master expresses keen disappointment. "Have I been with you disciples so long, and yet you, Philip, have not recognized me? Whoever has seen me has seen the Father. . . . You must believe me that I am in union with the Father and that the Father is in union with me" (vv. 9-10). Furthermore, says Jesus: "I am not saying these things on my own authority, but the Father who always remains in union with me is doing these things himself (v. 10).

In this and other passages our Lord declares himself one with God and urges his followers to accept him for what he claims to be. He feels impelled to press upon them in this last hour the absolute necessity of their believing that he comes from the Father and of their believing *in him* in simple trust. In spite of it, however, he feels a great sense of loneliness as he realizes that they will all soon be scattered in flight. "And yet I am not alone," he says, "because the Father is with me" (16:32). Then his own courage comes quickly so that he can comfort them with the words: "Be courageous! I have conquered the world" (v. 33). No conqueror ever spoke more truly.

Better to Go Away

Yet it is nothing but the truth I now tell you, that it is better for you that I should go away. For if I do not go away, the Helper will not come into close fellowship with you, but if I do go away, I will send Him to be in close fellowship with you (John 16:7).

Jesus realizes that his disciples must share his own experience of God or his ministry among them will come to naught. His insistence on this grows as the end of his earthly ministry draws near. It will not suffice for the disciples to remain dependent on his strength and on the inspiration of his physical presence. As long as he is with them they do indeed draw spiritual strength from him. But the very force of his character causes them to lean on him, to act only on his initiative and direction. Jesus realizes that unless he is gone from their physical presence they will never appropriate to themselves that vital quality which he has to give them. He wants them to have that sense of union with himself which he has with his Father in heaven. The essence of it, however, is personal experience. Each believer must have the thrill of discovery, the joy of finding out, the deep satisfaction of

knowing. Such knowledge does not come to one secondhand.
When we really know something, we know it from personal
experience.

I believe that Christ in his divine wisdom understands the
necessity of such personal independence in spiritual life. He has
shown his disciples how to live the godly life; he has revealed the
secret, demonstrated the power, infused them with the joy of it.
He has given them the keys to the kingdom of God. Now they
must learn to use the keys. They can only learn by doing. The
kingdom of God can only be lived by living it. They are now in
middle age. They will need all the time left them if they are to live
out the teachings of the Master in this life. I wonder if his own
death at about thirty-three is not made easier for our Lord by the
knowledge that by his leaving he is making it possible for them
to live out their normal span of years in a spiritual maturity which
could not have been theirs otherwise. So he tells them: "It is
better for you that I should go away."

We cannot fail to note the promise which accompanies this
announcement—the promise of a Comforter. The *Good News
Bible* reads "the Helper." "I will send him to be in close
fellowship with you," says Jesus. Shortly thereafter he says
again: "When the Spirit of truth comes, He will guide you into
the whole truth. . . . He will take the things that are mine and
tell them to you." Thus by the mystical aid of the Spirit those
who believe are enabled to share what Jesus has. He makes a
special point of saying that what the Spirit gives to us is not
merely what he, the Son, has to give, but what God the Father
has and is. "Everything that the Father has is mine; this is why I
have told you, 'He will take the things that are mine and tell
them to you.' "

Always Jesus insists that he is doing nothing of his own
power or for his own glory, but as the representative of his
Heavenly Father. Yet in the same breath he will make a claim of

supreme status for himself as God's own Son who shares everything with the Father. This amazing claim seems as natural to Jesus as it is for him to recognize his earthly parents as father and mother. Never does he assume an attitude such as: I know this seems incredible and I can hardly believe it myself, but I really am God's Son. No, Jesus makes no apology for his claim to sonship. He expects people to accept him and not only believe him but also believe *in* him. The only way anyone can reach that position is by faith, just as it is today. Christ wants it exactly that way. He cannot become the world's Savior on the basis of human logic. God cannot be contained in man's reason.

Perhaps our Lord has that in mind when he says to the twelve: "It is better for you that I should go away." It is not enough for them to believe, even believe *in* him, as a natural person. They must believe in him as Lord and Savior, a spiritual presence who is one with God. For that reason he has to leave them—by way of the cross.

God's Echo

Jesus said to them, "If God really were your Father, you would love me, because I came from God and now I am here. I did not come on my own authority, but he sent me. Why do you not understand what I say? It is because you cannot bear to listen to my message. You are the children of your father, the Devil, and you want to follow your father's desires. From the very beginning he was a murderer and has never been on the side of truth, because there is no truth in him. When he tells a lie, he is only doing what is natural to him, because he is a liar and the father of all lies. But I tell the truth, and that is why you do not believe me. Which one of you can prove that I am guilty of sin? If I tell the truth, then why do you not believe me? He who comes from God listens to God's words. You, however, are not from God, and that is why you will not listen" (John 8:42-47, GNB).

Jesus' self-assurance concerning his relation to God is amazing. Here is a man coming before a people noted for their religious background and claiming to have the special favor of God. He tells them that God is his Father and has revealed to him the truth, that this truth is embodied in himself, and that they must accept him and believe in him in order to have eternal life. "I am the living water," he says. "I am the light of the world." "I am the door." "I am from above." "I existed before Abraham was born." "I am the bread of life." "I am the resurrection and the life." "I am in union with the Father." "The Father and I are one."

He asserts that he does nothing except as God is working through him. He considers himself God's echo, simply repeating what God speaks, and he never has the slightest doubt about what God tells him to say or do. "I tell you the truth: the Son can do nothing on his own; he does only what he sees his Father doing. What the Father does, the Son also does" (John 5:19, GNB). Thus, while making the most extreme claims for himself, Jesus at the same time declares his absolute dependence on God. He feels that he is utterly helpless by himself, and yet with God's help he can prevail over anything or any power whatever. He is content to allow people to do what they will with him because he knows that they are unable to destroy that which is really vital, namely, the confidence which the Father has in him and the values inherent in that relationship.

To the Jewish leaders all this profession on the part of Jesus is brazen and presumptuous. Indeed it is worse than presumption, worse even than sacrilege. It is blasphemy, the most serious of all crimes in the Jewish code. Why do they respond to Christ's message with such intolerance and hate? Because they are fundamentally incapable of understanding it. They are unable to comprehend spiritual truth. They cannot grasp the concept of life which Jesus represents. "Why do you not understand what I say?" (GNB), he asks them, and then gives the answer: "It is because you cannot bear to listen to my message" (v. 43, GNB). "You, however, are not from God, and that is why you will not listen" (v. 47b, GNB). They have simply lost the capacity to understand spiritual matters, if indeed they ever had it.

In view of such claims for himself Jesus should be concerned to show the most convincing evidence available. From our human standpoint he should be expected to "prove" from Scripture or other means the validity of his claims. Such validation he refuses to offer. He simply tells people that he is the living Bread and urges them to "believe in" him, which means more than merely intellectual acceptance. It means to trust him and, by entering into his life, to come to know the Father. In the final analysis, then, the credential which Jesus offers for himself consists of the *experience* which one has *after* he has accepted Christ *on faith*. We accept him at his own self-appraisal, then through the unexplainable experience of "conversion" we enter into a mystical union with him, a relationship with unlimited possibilities in spiritual adventure and growth. As we continue to grow, his Father becomes our Father too.

Thy Will

My Father, if it is possible, let this cup pass by me; and yet, I pray, not what I want but what you want (Matt. 26:39b).

The hours spent in the garden on that last night are hours of darkness in every sense. The distress of soul experienced by the Master is hard to imagine. True, thousands have passed such a night awaiting their day of execution, being held in physical chains or behind bars of society's making. But Jesus is held only by the chains of his own dedication, by his sense of duty, by an utter devotion to God's will. He could have escaped. All the plausible reasons for it must have occurred to him, reasons which ordinary people would have grasped eagerly and rationalized as the will of God.

The plan of the cross was comprehended by Jesus long before. He has not only accepted it but has sought earnestly to prepare his disciples for it. Having accepted the cross as God's plan for him he walks steadfastly to meet it. But now as the dedication is about to become reality, here in the hour of final decision he recoils at the horrible prospect—yet goes on. His humanity is manifest in his desire to escape the cup. His divinity asserts itself in the greater desire to do his Father's will. It is that consciousness of God as "My Father" which carries him through, that and the conviction that God's will is revealed in the Scriptures. Three times he observes that the Scriptures are verified by what is taking place at Gethsemane.

Thus, in submission to God's will Christ wins the victory on the cross. Is that not the essential element in the atonement? The writer of Hebrews says that "it is by the will of God that we are consecrated through the offering of Jesus' body once for all" (Heb. 10:10). Christ's submission to God's will makes the atonement possible.

Darkness

As soon as day came, the elders of the people, the high priests, and the scribes assembled, and brought Him back before their council (Luke 22:66).

So Jesus came outside, still wearing the crown of thorns and the purple coat. Then Pilate said to them, "Here is the man!" (John 19:5).

The arrest and trial of Jesus is filled with drama. It is replete with satire, farce, tragedy, and mystery. It is a fast-moving story—the summons in the dead of night, a slight altercation with swords, the ignominious flight of the disciples, brutal treatment of Christ at the hands of thugs and henchmen, a farcical trial in the dimness of early morning. Meanwhile, a personal crisis overtakes Peter—a humiliating experience which cuts deep but transforms his life. With daybreak comes the necessity of bringing the proceedings into the open and prevailing upon the Roman authorities to give way. Some of the forms of law are observed, but the Roman trial becomes mainly a mob scene in which, as Luke says, "their shouts began to prevail," and Pilate allows the famed Roman justice to be made a hollow mockery.

In the various Gospel accounts there are numerous incidents which carry significance in themselves. John remembers that when the officers and their motley crew of followers arrive in the garden, Jesus steps forward and asks, "Who is it you are looking for?" and they answered "Jesus of Nazareth." People followed Jesus for years, trailed him from city to city, and searched for him when he withdrew to pray. Now they are seeking him again. But this time with an evil purpose. Evil people do not go looking for Jesus today, they avoid him. The world discovered that to search him out is to give him the victory. Those who have a hand in the arrest of Jesus unknowingly lead him out into the spiritual arena where he will vanquish the forces of darkness. They escort him to victory.

During the years of his ministry, Christ delayed for good reasons any public proclamation of his messiahship. The closing weeks, however, see several instances when he openly refers to himself as the Son of God. Now, during the trial, he is asked this crucial question, "Art thou the Christ?" He answers firmly, "I am." Before the morning is ended he responds likewise to the question which concerns the Roman governor, Pontius Pilate: "Are you the king of the Jews?" Jesus answers Pilate, "My kingdom does not belong to this world." (John 18:33,36). Thus the Lord Jesus who resolutely rejected the idea of a temporal kingship when his followers once tried to thrust it on him, now acknowledges the title, but only according to his own definition. His kingdom is not of this world. He remains true to the last to the spiritual pattern of his message and mission on earth.

John recalls that the Jews who bring Jesus to Pilate "would not go into the governor's palace themselves, in order not to be defiled, so as to be unfit to eat the Passover supper. So Pilate came outside" (John 18:28-29a). Here is an ironic climax to the running fight they have waged with Jesus over the strict observance of the law. They are determined to have this Jesus put to death for breaking the law, yet they are almost forced to break it themselves in the process of carrying out their evil purpose. Fortunately for their legal consciences, Pilate comes outside to them. The irony of the situation must not have been lost on these ceremonial-minded religionists as the bitter conflict over law and ritual comes to plague them almost to the very cross where they hoped to make an end of the matter.

It is also interesting to read that Pilate, after a brief interchange of words with the crowd, "went back into the governor's palace and called Jesus." Thus Jesus is ceremonially defiled according to the law. Would not he have considered this a suitable gesture with which to close the argument? His ministry has been dedicated to breaking the grip of legalism on people's minds and hearts. It is appropriate at this time that Jesus rather than his accusers should break the law.

Symphony of Hope

When the sabbath had ended, Mary of Magdala, Mary, James's mother, and Salome bought spices to go and anoint Him. It was very early, just after the sun had risen on the first day of the week, when they went to the tomb (Mark 16:1-2).

The women come to the tomb on Easter morning looking for the dead body of Christ. But they do not find it there in the tomb, nor will they ever find it in any particular place. The men in shining robes say to them: "Why do you look among the dead for him who is alive?" If we look for Jesus today in the tomb of history, he is not there; the historical Jesus is not the Jesus whom we know. We will find him in the present, not in history; in life, not in a tomb. True, the historical record provides us with understanding; without it we cannot comprehend him. But history cannot hold him in custody. Jesus Christ is a present reality. We do not look for him in a tomb.

The women are told by the angel that they need not be afraid. How often does Jesus utter the words, "Be not afraid." Here again we meet them as though given by proxy, the first words spoken by the angel to the women. Since Christ lives, fear vanishes. If we really have no fears in our lives, what joy and happiness are ours! No circumstance of life can cause uneasiness or distress if we are free from fear. Even pain and suffering lose their power when fear is conquered.

The women are urged also to go quickly and tell the disciples. The message of Jesus must be told or it becomes powerless. That is because it is a personal message to the individual heart. "Go and tell" is a vital part of the resurrection message. Thus do people hear that Christ is a living Christ.

What a message it is which the women are given to carry

back to the disciples! Can anything be more exciting? What joyful news for the little band of discouraged and fearful followers! It is "good news," a gospel of hope and cheer. The words which the angel speaks at the empty tomb echo the joyful song of the angels who sang at the birth of this same Jesus. It is a glad message, the same kind which announced the kingdom of God in the beginning. It has come full circle. The note of exuberant joy which characterizes Jesus' early ministry blends now with the deep overtones of suffering and triumphant pain, and breaks forth in a symphony of hope for all humankind. The Christ of the joyous life has suffered. The kingdom of God receives its full meaning.

Believing Is Seeing

Jesus said to him, "Is it because you have seen me, Thomas, that you believe? Blessed be those who believe, even though they have not seen me!" (John 20:29).

"Seeing is believing," according to an old saying. It is so with the disciples after the resurrection of the Lord Jesus. When they first heard about it from the women who returned from the empty tomb, it seemed to them to be nonsense and they would not believe them (see Luke 24:11). They had not yet seen him. But on the evening of that sabbath day Jesus comes in and stands among them and speaks to them. Then they believe *because they see him*.

Thomas is not there, however, and will not believe when the others tell him that they have seen the Master. A week later he, too, sees—and believes. Christ's words on this occasion are significant: "Is it because you have seen me, Thomas, that you believe? Blessed be those who believe, even though they have not seen me." Once again Jesus invokes a high spiritual law and beckons them to rise up to it. They believed because they saw him with their physical eyes. He turns it around and asks them to believe and then they will see him with spiritual eyes. Then he will become real to them. Just as he said in effect to the people before his crucifixion: if necessary, believe me because of my works, the wonders I perform, and other external evidence, but why not just accept me for what I am? So now he appeals to the disciples to accept him in faith as the risen Lord. He even seems to place a greater approval on those "who believe, even though they have not seen me."

Now, after many centuries, Christ is still asking us to believe in him. Believing without having seen him in the flesh, we too "see" him in that he is real to us and we are deeply aware of him. Hence, for us the proverb is reversed: Believing is seeing. We first accept him in faith and trust, then we "see" him as we experience him in our lives. Indeed, I am persuaded that the Savior may be *more* real to us as companion and friend than he was to those first disciples when they beheld his physical presence for a few fleeting days after the resurrection. Even in their own later experience it is with the coming of the Holy Spirit and the opening of their minds to many things that they truly "see" him—comprehend him—as they were not able to do when he was with them in the flesh.

Thus it is that we are able to share the experience of Christ with those who knew him in his earthly days. "Blessed be those who believe, even though they have not seen me." How are we blessed? We are blessed in that he is more real to us when seen through the eyes of faith and spiritual insight than any other way. We know him as the risen Christ because he lives within our hearts. Freed from the limitations of earthly life he stands forth in the clear sunshine of spiritual reality, calling us upward to the higher plane. With the eyes of the Spirit we behold him. Having believed, we see him. He comes now to minister to us and lead us forward in the kingdom of God.

Our Father, we bow in humble reverence before thee as we consider the mystery of thy power and the depths of thy love. We thank thee for the blessed experience of this spiritual journey. May our journey never end. Let the days of our earthly pilgrimage flow on in that timeless realm where thou doest reign supreme. Let us explore the kingdom of God forever. In the name of our Savior, Jesus Christ our Lord. Amen.